Endorsements for
Invisible to Viral

"As an author who embarked on this journey later in life, I intimately understand the challenges of sharing hard-earned wisdom with a wider audience. Michael Stickler's 'Invisible to Viral' is a game-changer for aspiring authors at any stage. Through John Larsen's compelling fictional journey, Mike masterfully illuminates the path from entrepreneurial success to literary acclaim. This book not only guides you through the intricacies of writing and publishing but also inspires you to persevere in the face of obstacles. Mike's expertise shines through, offering invaluable insights that extend beyond the page. For anyone with a story to tell or knowledge to share, 'Invisible to Viral' is your first step towards turning your invisible dream into a viral reality. It's more than a book—it's a roadmap to authorial success that I wish I'd had when I started my own writing journey."

Reinhard Klett, CHPC™
Certified High Performance Coach™
Author / TEDx -Speaker

"So, you want to right a book and you want to know what it takes. It's an adventure in and of itself to bring your dream to life. Thankfully for you, it's captured in a compelling adventure that is now a novel. 'Invisible to Viral' takes you on journey that may actually be yours. It's not just a fun read; it's a read that unlocks an opportunity hundreds of authors have taken before you!"

Terry Paulson, PhD,
Psychologist, Columnist,
Author of *The Summit.*

'Invisible to Viral'...is the journey of an entrepreneurial, successful businessman and his struggles with the complexities of the 'writing/publishing' world. This book is a great road map through the pitfalls and realities of 'vision' to realization!! A must read for the aspiring, developing, and even 'master' author!

Naomi Rhode, CSP, CPAE Speaker Hall of Fame
Past President National Speakers Association
Past President Global Speakers Federation
Author, Speaking and Life Coach
Co-Founder SmartHealth

"I became a New York Times bestselling author in 2004, ten years after commercially publishing my first book, which landed on many other bestseller lists. Last year, I met Michael Stickler through a God thing. With 15 commercially published books in my bibliography, published in 24 languages, I was astonished to learn from Mike how much the publishing industry has shifted beneath my feet. I asked if I could work with him and his team at Leadership Books for my next two projects. Mike is the wisdom and knowledge librarian of all that is book and media publishing in our mod- ern world. Now, you can access his vast knowledge and wisdom in his masterpiece of an aspiring writer's journey in Mike's new book, Invisible to Viral. I was a business person with a powerful message to share when I first published commercially. With Invisible to Viral, Mike has absolutely cracked the code on how to make the transition from business person to best selling author. As you turn each page in Invisible to Viral, re-member that each step of John Larsen's fictional publish-ing pilgrimage is based in real-life, real-time truth about how you, too, can successfully move from your current publishing aspirations to literary success."

"As an author who embarked on this journey later in life, I intimately understand the challenges of sharing hard-earned wisdom with a wider audience. Michael Stickler's 'Invisible to Viral' is a game-changer for aspiring authors at any stage. Through John Larsen's compelling fictional journey, Mike masterfully illuminates the path from en-trepreneurial success to literary acclaim. This book not only guides you through the intricacies of writing and publishing but also inspires you to persevere in the face of obstacles. Mike's expertise shines through, offering in-valuable insights that extend beyond the page. For anyone with a story to tell or knowledge to share, 'Invisible to Viral' is your first step towards turning your invisible dream into a viral reality. It's more than a book—it's a roadmap to authorial success that I wish I'd had when I started my own writing journey."

John Robert
John Hoover, PhD, MCC, MFT

Invisible to Viral

A Book Publishing Fable

Michael L. Stickler
with **Amanda Logan**

Most Leadership Books products are available at special quantity discounts for bulk purchases for sales promotions, premiums, fund-raising and educational needs. For details visit our website at www.leadershipbooks.com

Invisible to Viral by Michael L. Stickler
Published by Leadership Books, Inc.
Las Vegas, Nevada & New York, NY

Cataloging-in-Publication Data is on file with the Library of Congress.
International Standard Book Number:
ISBN: 978-1-951648-43-5

While the author has made every effort to provide accurate internet addresses at the time of publication, neither the publisher nor the author assumes any responsibility for errors or for changes that occur after publication. Further, the publisher does not have any control over and does not assume any responsibility for the author or third-party website or their content.

This is a work of fiction. Unless otherwise indicated, all the names, characters, businesses, places, events, and incidents in this book are either the product of the Author's imagination or used in a fictitious manner. Any resemblance to actual persons, living or dead, or actual events is purely coincidental.

Printed in the United States of America

Table of Contents

CHAPTER ONE

A Reluctant Author

John had never thought of himself as much of a writer. He was a business guy, not a book guy. In his 30-year career as an entrepreneur, he'd started and sold various successful businesses. In fact, he considered himself somewhat of an expert when it came to making a good exit strategy. His friends and family often told him that he should write a book on all his experience, but he didn't even know where to start with something like that. He'd written his share of essays in college, and of course, his career required some level of skill in writing proposals and other relevant documents, but book writing seemed like a whole other level.

Besides, life was good right now. He'd just sold another business. Both of his children were out of the house, the elder living a city over with a great job in marketing, and the younger attending a state college three hours away. He had his wife Margaret had become empty-nesters, and they were enjoying the extra time with each other. John hoped to use some of the money from his most recent exit to take Margaret on a trip, somewhere tropical or European. In any case, the book idea remained comfortably in the back of his mind, a "someday" project. He'd like it to happen, but he wasn't in any rush to make it happen.

That was until "the question."

The question came on a day like any other. John had been called in to tie up some loose ends of the business sale, so he'd driven in to the office to talk to the new owner. The conversation didn't take long, and as he was halfway out of the building when he heard hurried footsteps behind him.

"Sir!"

John turned around to see a young man in a crisp black suit and a matching tie, tightened almost to the point of strangling. He couldn't have been more than 25 years old. John could practically smell the new business degree on him.

The young man slowed his step, panting a little as he got closer. Had he run down the stairwell to catch him?

"Excuse me, sir," he said, sticking out his hand. "My name is Brian Anderson."

"Nice to meet you, Brian," John said, accepting the handshake. "What can I do for you?"

"Well," Brian suddenly looked a little timid. "I was only hired on recently, but I've heard a lot about your accomplishments in business. I'm working here now, but I'd really like to start up my business one day."

"That's a wonderful goal."

"Thank you." Brian smiled at the ground before abruptly correcting himself to look back at John. "I, uh, I was wondering if I could ask you something." He plucked his pen from his breast pocket and fished out a small pad of orange sticky notes. John wondered if he'd grabbed them hastily off his desk before going after him.

"Of course," John said.

"Ok, uh," Brian took a deep breath. "If you could share 5 secrets to your success, what would they be?"

John paused. "Wow, that's a good question." He sifted rapidly through his past experiences and knowledge. He had plenty of things he could share with a new start-up, but in this moment, he couldn't seem to pin down anything specific. Maybe because there was too much he wanted to share. Out of all of it, what was the most important?

"My secrets to success, huh?" he stalled.

Brian stood at the ready, pen tip pressed to the first sticky note.

Come on, John. Think of something clever. Something inspiring.

"First, I have to say, never give up. Starting a business is hard work. So when things get tough, don't give up." John cringed a little at the repetition.

"Never…give…up," Brian echoed under his breath as he wrote. He looked back up. "Ok."

Not a great start, but there were still four more tips that could make this conversation meaningful. If he could just think of one. He seized onto the first thought to cross his mind. "Next, always do your research."

"On the competition?" Brian asked. "Or on the demand for the product?"

"Both. All of it. Anything that may affect the business's success or how it runs." That was too vague. He should probably give more examples of what exactly those things might be, but it felt like too much to explain. There were many, many factors that one had to research to make their business successful. Brian could probably infer a lot of them on his own, and he didn't want to ramble, so he continued, "Then of course you need to be passionate about whatever you're doing. Otherwise, you're not going to enjoy your work. How many is that so far?

"Uh, three, I think," Brian said. "Don't give up, do research, be passionate."

John's insides twisted hearing it all together. It was such basic advice; it could apply to practically anything. Brian had probably heard all of it in his classes already. He needed to tell this kid something good, something that would actually make a difference in his business career. "You know, it's very important to 'ask why'?"

"Ask why?"

"Yes, *why* are you creating the business you're creating?'" That advice was closely linked to research and being passionate, but maybe it would like help Brian think when it came to any future business endeavors. "Finally, be sure to count your costs too."

Brian scribbled it down. "Yeah, I'm sure you'd have to keep track of your spending when you're starting off."

"I mean your personal costs," John said.

"Oh. Right." Brian hesitated and then wrote something else down. John suspected it probably read something like "Count costs – personal?"

"Personal costs are things like time, emotional wellbeing, even family. You need to decide how much you're willing to sacrifice for your business."

"*Oh.*" The young man hastily crossed out the previous note and rewrote it. "Yeah, that makes sense."

They stood in silence for a moment, Brian looking expectant, and John trying to think of more to say. That was five pieces of advice, but he didn't feel satisfied with his answers. These were only scratches on the surface; he had experiences to share, pitfalls to avoid, deeper explanations to make his current points more meaningful. He wanted to share more, but all he could think of now were stories. There were nuggets of wisdom in each of them, but it was a lot to get into right now when the young man probably needed to get back his job.

"Well, thank you for the tips," Brian said finally.

Tips. Not the five secrets to success, just tips. Perhaps the man didn't mean anything by it, but John couldn't help but feel disappointed in himself for giving such underwhelming advice.

"Of course," John replied.

Brian hesitated a moment longer then flicked out a business card from the inside pocket of his suit. It was still a very simple thing, only a name, a phone number, and an email.

"You're probably way too busy, but, uh, could you let me know if you think of anything else?"

"I'll be sure to do that," John said.

Brian nodded, and with that, headed back to work—this time he took the elevator.

That evening at dinner, John related the whole embarrassing event to Margaret. If anyone would be honest with him, it was her. She had always been his greatest support. In the early days of his career, he'd spent many hours outside of the home with very little fruit in return, but she'd remained stalwart through it all, encouraging him through his failures and setting his priorities straight when he focused too hard on work. Now that the kids had moved away, she was still his greatest constant.

"I felt like an idiot," John said, pushing his peas around on his plate.

"You were put on the spot," Margaret said. "Anyone would struggle to know what to say in a situation like that."

"Except I had the answers! I just couldn't seem to get them out. It was like there were so many things that I wanted to tell him that I couldn't explain any of them. He could have googled a better answer."

"From what you told me, you didn't do all that bad. Besides, it isn't your responsibility to advise people. You didn't go in prepared to talk about your business strategy, so you can expect to give all the perfect answers."

"I know, I know." John stabbed a few of the peas on his fork but still felt too riled to eat them. "But the kid was a fresh graduate, looking for direction. I know how that is. He probably thought he could get better answers straight from the source, but I don't think I gave him anything worthwhile." He sighed. "I wish I could redo it."

Margaret set down her fork, meeting John's eyes across the table. "What is this really about?"

"What do you mean?"

"I mean is this really about embarrassing yourself in front of a stranger you'll never see again or is there something more to it?"

That was just like her. Margaret always could see straight through his pretenses, sometimes even before he saw them himself.

"I don't know." John rubbed his hand over his face. "I guess I just feel like I've been blessed. I'm proud of my work; I'm proud of everything we've achieved. We're in a great place now, but I remember what it was like before I hit my stride, back when I wished someone could give me a secret to success to make things easier. I'd like to give some of what I've learned back. Help others find success."

Margaret took his hand. "And that is wonderful. But you can't beat yourself up over one bad conversation. You'll do better next time."

John started to nod but then shook his head instead. "If someone were to ask me again tomorrow, I still don't know if I could give them the right answers. There are so many pieces to my success, I think I'd need several hours to share it all."

"Or a book," Margaret said.

John blinked. "What?"

"A book. You know, the one you keep saying that you're going to write. Why not now?"

John *had* said he wanted to write a book. But saying it and doing it were two very different things. He didn't even know where to begin. Not only was writing a long process, but he didn't know anything about publishing. Part of why he'd put it off for so long was because he knew he'd have to address all those things, and it felt, well, *intimidating*.

And yet, the idea was so perfect. A book was a medium that reached many people. It would also allow him to delve deeper into his experiences and explain all the details of his process. In a book, he could distill his ideas in a way that would actually help people.

"Alright." His heart skipped a bit as he committed out loud. "I'm going to write a book. A good one."

Despite his unfamiliarity, having a plan brought some immediate comfort. Now all he needed to do was figure out how to start, and he knew someone who could help.

Dr. Richard P. Harbrook had worked as an English professor at the local college for as long as John had known him. He taught the undergrad students in the afternoon and the graduate students in the evening, but he was rarely satisfied with the work of either. He also happened to be John's next-door neighbor. Though Richard came off a bit pretentious on the first meeting, John respected his dedication to his craft, and from the way he rambled on about literature, he certainly knew a lot more about book writing than John did.

Richard and his wife Alice were hosting a neighborhood barbecue in the upcoming week, so John seized that opportunity to speak to Richard about the book idea.

When they arrived, John only took enough time to set the potato salad on the table with the rest of the food before scanning the yard for Richard. He quickly spotted him on the other side of the yard on grill duty.

"Hey, Richard," he greeted.

"John," Richard acknowledged without looking up from the grill. "I'm glad you two could make it."

"Of course, we always look forward to coming over." He paused. "Hey, I was wondering if I could pick your brain about something?"

Richard spared him a glance. "I suppose I can flip and listen at the same time."

"I want to write a book."

"I wouldn't recommend it," Richard said.

The blunt response took John aback. He had figured Richard would be excited that he was taking interest in his craft. He wasn't exactly sure how to respond, so he watched Richard fastidiously flip a couple of burgers before finally asking, "Why not?"

"These days everyone is writing a book. Everyone thinks they can be a writer, but the truth is that a very small percentage of those people get published, and an even smaller percentage has any success. Forgive my bluntness, John, but you're not a writer. If you're writing for yourself that's wonderful, but if your goal is publication, I wouldn't get my hopes up."

John frowned. This was not what he'd wanted to hear. If Richard didn't think it was possible, a part of him didn't see the point in pushing it further, but he'd also never been the type of person to give up before really trying. "Don't you think I should give it a try before deciding it's impossible?"

Perhaps there was something in John's tone because Richard finally tore his gaze away from the grill. His face softened a bit. "I'm sorry, John. I have a hundred students telling me every day they're writing books, and they all think they're going to be the world's next bestselling author. I often have to be brutally honest with them about what the industry is really like. Of course, there is no harm in trying. What is your book about?"

Richard's rudeness had John a little annoyed, but this was what he was here for, so he tried to brush it off. "It's a book on business. I want to share my experiences in both starting and selling businesses, and I want to advise others on how they can do the same."

Richard hummed thoughtfully. "Well, if it's that sort of book, I suppose it's not hopeless. You are a professional in that area after all. Have you written anything yet?

"Not yet. That's what I wanted to talk to you about. Where should I begin? How does one go about being published?"

"There's no one way to begin writing," Richard said, scooping four burgers one after the other onto a waiting cookie sheet. "Some people write chronologically; others write out of order. You do what works best for you. But when it comes to publishing, you're going to want to find an agent."

John knew about agents when it came to celebrities and move stars, but he hadn't realized that agents also applied to book writing. "Alright, what do they do?"

"They pitch your book to the publishers. If your book is published, they get a portion of what publishing company pays you."

John furrowed his brow. He may not have known much about publishing, but he did know about saving costs.

"Can't I just write the book and send it to a publisher myself?"

"Of course not," Richard scoffed.

John furrowed his brow even further. "And why not?"

"No publishing company will talk to you without an agent. If you do find a company that says that an agent isn't required, they'll still look at the agented manuscripts first. Yours might stay at the bottom of the submission pile forever."

"Ok, so how do I find an agent?"

"First, you have to come up with a pitch for your book, so that you can convince an agent you're worth working with. Once you're ready, you can find them on social media, publishing websites, writing conferences." He looked thoughtful. "The college hosts a writing conference every summer. I usually suggest it to my students when they want to learn more about publishing. There is a $30 entrance fee, but writers, editors and publishers come from all over to learn and give advice about publishing. It's a great place to network, so if you want to find an agent, that's a good place to start."

"Alright, I'll look into that." John had attended many business and marketing events, so he knew firsthand how helpful they could be both socially and informationally. Research was key to success, and John certainly had a lot of questions. Maybe they could help him to know how to begin writing as well.

"Would you like me to come with you?"

John's attention shot back to Richard. After all the negativity he'd offered, John hadn't been expecting him to offer any further help. Though he had to admit, it would be nice to have someone like Richard at the conference with him. Richard may have been brutally honest, but wasn't that what John needed right now? Besides, the professor had been to many writing conferences. It would be easier to find his way around and to find an agent with someone more experienced to help.

"That would be great, Richard, thank you."

Richard scooped the last of the burgers onto the cookie sheet and began heading toward the food table. "I wanted to go anyway. I'm giving my summer students extra credit for participating, so it's beneficial for me to hear what they'll be learning. Besides, you're going to need all the help you can get."

John strained a smile. "Thanks, Richard."

At least now he had a direction towards taking his first step.

CHAPTER TWO

The Literary "Rabbit Hole"

John hadn't known how big of an event to expect, but when he and Richard arrived at the college's English building, a sizeable crowd was already bustling through the halls.

"Welcome to the conference," chirped the woman behind the admission's table. "What are your names?"

"John Larsen," John said.

"Richard Harbrook."

She sifted through the little box of name tags in front of her. "Ah, here we are!" She handed them their badges and waved to the rows of plastic bags on her left. "Go ahead and grab a bag. They all have a building map, conference schedule, and a lanyard for your name badge inside. There are also a couple of coupons for some of the books being sold in the vendor room. Enjoy!"

They briefly thanked her, before heading to an open space against the wall to look over the map and schedule. There appeared to be simultaneous panels in about a dozen lecture halls. The vendor room was set up in the common area on the first floor, and a few writing workshops were scattered throughout the day in other open classrooms.

"When I come to these events, I circle anything that looks interesting," Richard said, pen already out. "You have to prioritize the most important." He sighed as he scanned the first time slot. "So many panels on genre fiction this year. 'Dragons, Dragons, and More Dragons'? What sort of a panel title is that? Ridiculous."

John plucked out his own pen, running the tip lightly down the bulleted list.

10:00 am

- Rm. 102 – Dragons, Dragons, and More Dragons
- Rm. 103 – Worldbuilding 101
- Rm. 104 – Editing
- Rm. 105 – 10 Tips to Publishing

"10 Tips to Publishing, that sounds interesting." One of John's biggest hang-ups on this book thing was his unfamiliarity with publishing. Right now, the process felt dark and nebulous. It would be nice to hear other people's takes on the subject and hopefully get some of his questions answered.

Richard pursed his lips. "Well, it's certainly the most helpful panel going on this hour."

A few minutes later, they arrived at Room 105. The first couple rows were already full, but the room was built in an auditorium style though, so John didn't mind grabbing a couple of open seats in the middle rows. Once they were both seated, John pulled out a notebook from his bag and laid his pen across the first page in anticipation for the class to begin. To his surprise, rather than an entire panel of speakers, only one person sat at the front of the room, a thin, bald man with a cheery smile peeking out from under his mustache. The man eagerly watched the remaining people filter in, as if he could hardly contain himself from sharing his knowledge.

Within a few minutes, the audience had settled, and the man strode across the room to close the door.

"Good morning, everyone," he boomed, the portable microphone forgotten on the desk. "I'm glad to see that so many people decided to come to my class when there is a panel about dragons down the hall."

The whole room chuckled.

"My name is Mitch Robinson, and I am an author, editor, and writing coach. I've worked both freelance and for a multitude of publishing companies, and throughout my years in the publishing industry, I have found one of the biggest concerns for an author, no matter their experience level, is publishing. Now, this isn't the type of lesson where I'm going to debate publishing methods or give you a step by step on how to submit your manuscript to companies. There are plenty of panels on those topics here already. Today, I want to teach you the baseline to being a great author.

"Now, we usually have a Q and A at the end of each panel, but I know how easy it is to forget a question when you're learning new information, so feel free to raise your hand at any point."

Mitch uncapped a dry erase market laying underneath the white board and wrote a large number one, followed by the word "passion." He turned back toward the audience.

"The first thing I enforce in new authors, or even experienced authors, is that they must be passionate about their work. I want you to ask yourself, do you have a passion for the subject you are writing about? Are you passionate about your book's contents?"

John copied the first bullet point into his notebook. He could relate to this. As an entrepreneur, he'd found building a business was much more difficult when he didn't care about the product. A few weeks ago, he'd worried about sharing something so simple as one of his secrets to success, but suddenly, it didn't seem like such a lame piece of advice.

"Until that passion runs out," Richard scoffed from John's right. The professor leaned way back in his seat, arms folded in front of them. Though Richard had been the one to recommend John bring something to write notes in, he didn't have any notebook of his own on his fold out desk. When he noticed John looking at him, he whispered, "Passion is fleeting. People's interests change like dust in the wind. It's too unstable to be a base for a book."

"I've met many people, who try to write a book about what they *think* would be good," Mitch continued. "Maybe it's a topic that sounds important, or something popular they think will get them a lot of readers. But in the end, they can't sum up the motivation to finish their work because they don't really care about it. Or if they do finish, the writing is soulless. If that's not reason enough, being passionate about your book will guarantee that you will enjoy the writing process. Otherwise, writing can be a slog."

Mitch turned back to the board. "Number two: be a storyteller. This goes hand in hand with passion. When you first start writing your book, don't worry so much about 'how does it sound?', 'how will you market it?', 'will anyone like it?', and all those other intrusive questions. The only thing you need to worry about is telling a good story. Because ultimately, that's your job. When you enjoy the stories you're telling, the other things will fall into place."

Richard's chair creaked as he straightened in his seat. "What sort of advice is that?" he hissed at John. "Being a storyteller doesn't make you writer. The market is flooded with mediocre books for that very reason. We're just supposed to believe in ourselves and magically everything will work out?"

Perhaps Mitch already had more to say, or perhaps he overheard Richard's comment because he continued calmly, "Of course, the quality of your writing matters later down the road, but when you're first getting started, over-worrying about it will only hinder you. You aren't expected to be perfect, especially not on a first draft. However, a reader can tell when the author put their heart into their work. If you neglect the story because you're concentrating on everything else, your readers will feel it."

He turned back to the board and wrote a number three under the two. "Speaking of readers, that brings us to our third point: be reader conscious.

"Whenever I'm coaching an author, one of my first questions is 'who are you writing for?'" Knowing the type of people you want to connect with will not only give your writing better direction, it will help you out with the marketing process later."

A blonde young woman in the front row slowly raised her hand.

He pointed to her with an encouraging smile. "Yes?"

"What if I'm writing a book meant for everyone?"

Mitch chuckled. "You're not the first person to ask me that. Many of the authors I've worked with have books that appeal to a wide demographic of people. But to be honest, you cannot expect everyone to like your book, and trying to cater to every person will only burn you out. You have to identify your target audience. An exercise I find helpful, is imagining your target audience as a single person. What type of person is this? What is their age? What are they interested in? Imagine yourself writing to that person."

John wrote under bullet point three, *Who is my reader?*

That part was simple. His book was about his entrepreneurial experience and strategy, so his target audience was other business leaders. He imagined Brian, who he had wanted to speak to with more clarity, and then pictured giving him the advice soon to be written in his book. Having an image of who he wanted to reach really did help him feel more confident.

"What a great question," Mitch said. He paused a moment in case any other hands went up. When none did, he went back to the board and wrote the fourth tip.

4. Market a need

"How is your book different from other books on the market? What makes *you* different from other authors writing on the same topic? Besides having passion for your book, you have to be aware of what the industry is lacking and what is in demand."

Mitch gestured, and John turned his head to see an older woman behind him lowering her hand. "I'm writing a non-fiction book about anthropology. I want to make young people think about human behavior and other cultures, but fiction is such a popular genre; I'm worried that not many people will be interested in a book like mine. I suppose what I'm asking, is how do you market a book like that, that is needed, without making it seem like a textbook?"

Mitch nodded along as she spoke and then paused for a moment to think. "When it comes to writing nonfiction, one helpful format I've found is creating a narrative. Stories keep readers engaged. It also helps them retain the information that you want to them to learn. So you might consider using your own stories, or creating a fictional narrative to relay your subject."

Another audience member raised his hand, this time a bearded man in his thirties.

"What if I have a premise for a story, but I don't know where I want to go with it yet? I'm worried that my idea might be too similar to books that are already published."

"That's a great question and perfect segway into our next tip." Mitch turned back to the board. "Number five: get your ideas down on paper. When you decide to write a book, one of the first things you should do, even before you start writing, is do a brain dump. Start writing down all your ideas, sketch out a plan. It doesn't have to be organized; you don't even have to include all of it in your book. But this process will get your creativity flowing and help you generate a lot of ideas for your story. As you come up with ideas, you'll be able to come up with ways to make your story unique."

"Finally, some practical advice," Richard muttered.

John frowned at his friend. Richard had recommended this conference to him, but he kept complaining about Mitch's advice. Was Mitch really so wrong? Or did Richard simply have different methods. John had assumed once he got to the conference everything would become clear, and these tips were helpful, but between two experienced professionals who was he supposed to believe?

"Number six," Mitch said, bringing John's attention back to him, "it takes a team. So many authors think they have to do it all on their own. Many of the people I've met are reluctant to write because they're frozen by fear. They don't know how to do it, so they don't do it at all. But publishing isn't a solo sport, it's a team sport. Once you realize this, you'll feel so much freer. You have editors, marketers, publishers, designers all here to help you with the stuff you don't know how to do. **Your job is to tell the story**.

"That being said, stay in your lane." Mitch wrote that instruction next to the number seven. "Storytelling is your job, so let the editors, designers, and marketers do their jobs. I know what it's like to be protective of your book. It's your baby. But for your book to be published effectively, you need to be able to let go and allow your team to help you."

Next, he wrote a number eight on the board.

"Once you've got your team and accepted your role in it, you can move on to tip number eight: be prepared to work hard. Publishing a book is hard. Don't let anyone tell you otherwise. There are plenty of articles out there that will make it seem easy or try to tell you there are shortcuts to making it easy, but any good book is going to take serious work. Know that the process takes time. Put in your best effort to write and then allow the others the time to do their work. You want your book to be as excellent as possible, and the greater the quality of your book the greater your sales are going to be. However, if you're only writing a book because you want to get rich, get that idea out of your head right now. Profit is important, but it's an outcome to quality storytelling. Your focus should be on creating a great book. This may take several rewrites, and by the end you may be sick of looking at it, but then you'll know that you've done everything you can to make your book excellent.

"Once the book is finished, you must move on to tip nine: have a platform for promotion. The success of your book depends on how well you promote it. It could be the best book ever written, but if nobody knows about it, they aren't going to buy it. Try to be involved in anything that will get your book seen, whether that be book signings, interviews, posting on social media or attending conferences like this one."

A man on the same row as John raised his hand. "How long do I have to promote my book? Shouldn't my publisher do that for me anyway?

"There are some companies that will come up with a marketing plan for you. But unfortunately, most companies, even the big ones, require you to market yourself. I recommend promoting your book the whole year after it's published. If you have other manuscripts you are working on, your published book should be a priority. Especially because your next books will have much smoother publications after your first one gains momentum. Any other questions?"

The crowd remained silent.

Mitch smiled. "That leaves us with our last tip: start working on your next book. We're all writers, so we tend to have a lot of ideas all at once. If you start getting ideas for another book while you're writing, take some notes and set them aside. Once your first book is finished, go ahead and pull those notes out again. You may be thinking right now, 'But Mitch, I only have one idea.' That may be so at the moment, but I promise, you always have another book inside of you."

From there the lesson continued with a brief Q and A session. John soaked in everything. He took extensive notes of everything that the people around him asked, and when their time ran out at 10:55am, instead of following Richard straight out the door, he approached Mitch as he erased the board.

"Excuse me, do you have a card I could look at?"

Mitch turned around; that warm smile was even more encouraging up close. "Of course." He reached into his front pocket and passed a card to John.

"Thank you. I enjoyed hearing your tips."

"I'm glad it had an impact on you," Mitch said.

John almost walked away then, but he stopped.

"I'm new to book writing and publishing, so perhaps this is a silly question, but what exactly is a writing coach?

"Not a silly question at all. In my case, it means I help authors reach their writing goals. That involves uplifting them, helping them brainstorm, and guiding them through each stage of the writing process."

Someone knocked on the door, and a woman with different colored name badge than the guests pointed at her watch.

"Ah," Mitch said, "I better clear out of the room before the next panel shows up, but please, contact me if you have any questions, or would like a consultation on your book."

"I will, thank you."

John exited into the hallway. Richard waited against the wall to the left of the doors. No sooner had John seen him than the professor began ranting. "That presenter was very idealistic, wasn't he? There are way more variables to publishing than he talked about. 'Publishing is a team sport,' yeah, if you can actually find a publishing company that will be a team to you. In my experience, you're book has to be great before you even speak to a publisher."

"So the tips were wrong?" John asked.

Richard faltered. "They weren't necessarily 'wrong'," he said. "But they aren't what *I* would suggest when it comes to publishing."

Then it *was* a matter of opinion. Richard had done little more than nitpick everything since arrival, so John found himself agreeing more with Mitch's perspective, but he didn't want to start a debate with Richard, especially over a subject that the professor was more knowledgeable about, so he simply said, "I'm sorry to hear that. Let's decide which panel to attend next. Is there something you think would be more beneficial?"

"There's a panel on classic literature I want to attend this hour; I don't think it will be very helpful for you. But the schedule shows there are pitching sessions for the next couple of hours in the second-floor common area. It would be a good opportunity to network. If you get the pitch right, you might even get yourself an agent."

Right, the agent. That was the main reason he was here today. He hoped whatever agent he found would be someone like Mitch, someone who would be able to guide him through both the writing and publishing process.

He and Richard split ways, and John made his way toward the stairs, opting for the ones at the end of the hall so that he could get a better look the events on the first floor.

People moved rapidly toward their next classes sweeping him along in their current. Everyone here seemed so passionate about writing, they clutched books and notepads and talked eagerly to each other about their current projects. John couldn't help but feel like an imposter. He'd only decided he wanted to write a few weeks ago. Did he really deserve to be here with all these people who had probably been writing for years now?

As they reached the end of the hall, the crowd gradually diverged, allowing John to escape its push. He now stood in the common area by the stairs. The room had been cleared, and long tables were set up in rows from the wall to the walkway. Each table was filled with books, bookmarks, pens, and other literary items while the respective authors stood on the other side, explaining the plot of their books to every passerby that lingered too long.

"Hello!"

John turned. A woman with a bright red bob sat at the nearest table. Several stacks of brightly colored books laid out in front of her along with a poster propped up on a display stand. It showed a bigger version of the book's cover: The Magician's Kiss by Betty Sanders

"Hello," John nodded politely.

"Do you or anyone you know have an interest in fantasy romance?" Before he could answer, she continued, "I currently have a sale, if you buy one book you get a second 50% off. They would make great gifts for birthdays or Christmas."

"I'm afraid I'm not much of a fantasy reader," John said. Suddenly a thought occurred to him. "It's impressive that you were able to publish though. Was it hard to get an agent?"

"Oh, I don't have an agent. I'm self-published." She gave a haughty smile. "In fact, I'm an Amazon bestseller."

"Really?" John hadn't thought about self-publishing before. Richard would probably tell him that self-publishing wasn't a valid publication, but as long as his book was able to help people, he didn't really mind how it was published. "How many books have you sold?"

"About 10 today, but I've sold over 100 online."

"When did you start self-publishing?"

Betty faked a smile. "About two years ago? I've published three books online already; this is just my newest release."

John's heart sank. That number seemed a little low. He wanted his book to reach a bigger audience than that. Was that really what it meant to be an Amazon bestseller? Perhaps self-publishing wasn't the best choice for him after all.

He chatted for a couple more minutes then politely excused himself, heading up the stairs into the connecting common area. This one still had its benches and chairs in the right spots, along with a couple small round tables where a couple people sat, typing on their laptops A few feet away, a young woman spoke at rapid speed about her book's plot while the older woman in front of her nodded along unenthusiastically. Looking around the room, almost everyone was speaking in pairs. John could tell the agents from the authors from the contrast in their dispositions. The authors were overly nervous, and the agents seemed tired. John wondered how many pitches they'd heard in the last hour alone.

Only one man seemed to be unoccupied, so John approached him first.

"Hello. I'm writing a book on building businesses and implementing exit strategies. Would you be interested in hearing more about it?"

"Excuse me," the man said. "I only accept pitches by appointment."

John frowned. He hadn't been aware that he needed an appointment in such an informal setting, but he didn't press further. He stepped back to wait for one of the other agents to be available. The next few conversations were similar. One agent had already met their quota of clients. Another didn't promote non-fiction. A third would only accept clients with completed manuscripts. All in all, John felt wholly unprepared.

After he'd spoken to most of the agents in the room, he was tempted to return downstairs for the remainder of the conference. Perhaps he would meet an agent later in the day. Or perhaps he could Google a few people online when he had more of his manuscript finished. But he didn't get to where he was by giving up, so he thought he should give it at least one more try.

The older woman he'd seen upon first entering the room had gone through several authors, but she now stood alone. She checked the time on her phone and started toward the staircase.

Channeling the confidence of his inner businessman, John quickly intercepted her, This time he went straight into his pitch.

"Excuse me, my name is John Larsen. I've spent 30 years as an entrepreneur and I'm writing a book about my experiences in building businesses and creating exit strategies. My goal is to help other businessmen achieve success. Do you have a few minutes to talk?"

The woman checked her phone again then glanced at the stairs. She seemed to want to say no, but she strained a smiled. "Rebecca Collins. I can spare a few moments. You're writing a book on business.

"Yes." John searched his mind for some of the points he'd learn in the class, anything to keep her attention. "I am very passionate about the topic and my years of experience make me a great candidate for advice. The market is in need of more books on business. With my many personal experiences, the book would be an engaging read that would give businessmen… and women a realistic visual on how to start a business."

"Do you have a complete manuscript you could send me?" Rebecca asked, some interest sparked in her eyes.

John cringed. "It's still in progress, but I can send you a few of the personal stories I plan to include."

The interest withered almost instantly.

"I can have a first chapter to you within the week if you like," he said. "I'm well-known in my field, so anyone can vouch for my work ethic."

Rebecca looked thoughtful. "Ok, fine, I'll bite. Usually, I expect a finished manuscript before taking on a client, but if you send me a sample of your writing within the next few days, I can see about taking you on. I often work with non-fiction authors, and with someone of your experience, I foresee a lot of success if the writing is good."

She reached into her purse and pulled out a card with her name typed above an illustration of a book; the backside contained her phone number and email. "Reach out to me when you get a chance."

John accepted the card. "Thank you, I'll be in touch."

An excited feeling rose in his chest. He was pretty sure he had an agent.

CHAPTER THREE

More No than Yes

John stared at the blinking cursor on the screen. Writing a first chapter was harder than he'd thought. He'd started several times over the last hour, but he never got further than a paragraph before deleting it all. Nothing flowed right. Every time he tried to put something on the page it either came off too stiff or too wordy. It didn't help that his insides were a constant whirl of anxiety. He needed to get this done as soon as possible.

Not long after the conference, John had written Rebecca a follow-up email. He had figured that the best way to stay on her radar was to put himself in her inbox. In the email, he had promised to send her a sample by the end of the week, which she had promptly agreed to. It was now Friday.

He sighed heavily, running his hands over his face. He had never been one to shirk a deadline, and he wasn't about to start now. He needed to buckle down and type something out. Even if his chances at getting published depended on the quality of his writing in this moment.

Should he begin with an introduction of himself, or should he begin with one of his business stories? Or maybe he should start by explaining one of his business principles.

After Mitch's class, he'd hoped that having an agent would grant him some guidance, but he couldn't tell Rebecca he had no idea what he was doing or else she would drop him.

He was stuck.

Eventually John minimized the document and pulled up a search bar on Google.

How to write a book, he typed.

The first results were simple things like "start with a hook," "decide what to write about," or "create a routine", but as John scrolled, he came across a page that read "5-step guide to creating an outline." Richard had mentioned some writers liked to outline, and it had also been mentioned a few times at the conference. Maybe if he started there, he could at least get some of his ideas out onto the page.

He began by listing all the experiences he wanted to include in the book as well as the main tips and principles. From there, he attempted to organize them into chapters. However, that proved problematic since he wasn't exactly sure how to order it all. He ended up reorganizing the information ten times before finally settling on something, but even then, he didn't feel confident in the placement. Part of the problem was transitioning from one topic to the next. It was hard to tell in an outline form whether the topic changes were too abrupt or if pieces of his book even belonged next to each other. Did he have too many stories in a row? Would it be strange to put several principles of his success in the same chapter? His owns doubts and questions bombarded him, but there didn't seem to be any real answer for him.

Eventually, he decided to move on, but the next challenge came when he tried to fill in the gaps. The outlining guide said to be as detailed as possible, but so much of his book still felt unknown to him. Did he really need to know *everything* before he could even begin writing? A part of him would rather just write and figure it out, but he also didn't want to waste any more time.

By the time he finished outlining, he actually felt more stressed. Though it was nice to have all the information in front of him, the excitement he'd felt about writing had diminished. Following a strict guide to writing—even if he'd made it himself—felt restricting and tedious. But maybe that was what writing was, and he just needed to be more disciplined.

A light knock on the door, jolted John out of his thoughts, and Margaret peeked into the room.

"How's it going in here?" she said, cracking the door open wider so she should lean against the door frame.

"It's going," John said, trying to keep his voice more upbeat than he felt.

Margaret raised her brows.

"It's…alright," John tried again. "I've made an outline. That's progress. I still haven't written the first chapter though. I didn't know how to start, but now I do. I think."

"You've been in here for hours," Margaret said. "Don't burn yourself out. Maybe you should take a break and eat something."

John shook his head. "I want to send this to the agent by tomorrow. I should at least get a first draft done."

Margaret didn't look like she agreed, but she nodded anyway. "How long does the first chapter have to be?"

"She didn't say, but I remember Mitch saying, 3,000 to 4,000 words is the average. If I start now, hopefully I can finish by dinner." Margaret nodded idly again, stepping further into the room to look over his shoulder at his computer screen. Her eyes scanned down the screen, John anxiously awaiting her reaction, but after a moment she simply said, "Just don't overthink it. You know what you're talking about, and you know what will help other people in your career."

John sighed. "Yes, but that might not be enough. Right now, it only matters what the agent thinks of my work. I need to prove to her that I can do this."

"You *can* do this," Margaret said, squeezing both his shoulders. "No matter what the agent ends up saying."

John smiled weakly. That was a nice sentiment, but not what he wanted to hear right now. After his experience with the agents at the conference, he couldn't guarantee he'd get another lucky break. He needed to seize this opportunity while he had it.

"Thank you, hon," he said. Then, when she didn't budge, "I promise I'm not burning myself out."

"Alright," she relented, moving back to the door. She shot him one last encouraging smile. "Good luck in here."

The door clicked shut behind her, and the room was quiet again. John's anxious thoughts, temporarily quieted by the conversation, worked back up into a frenzy.

I can do this, he thought to himself, reopening the Word document and hovering his fingertips over the keyboard. *I can do this.*

With that self-encouragement echoing in his mind, John started cranking out the first chapter to his outline. Sometimes it was slow and awkward since he didn't know all the grammar rules, and other times he worried whether the writing was good enough to impress Rebecca, but this time he tried to move forward anyway rather than delete it all when he was unsure. Though, every once in a while, his writing strayed from his outline, and he had to backtrack so that he didn't tell information out of order.

When he finished his brain felt fried, but he was proud to have 3,500 words in front of him. He scrolled back to the top of the document, intent on getting his revisions done quickly, but then he remembered Margaret's advice not to burn himself out. He probably could use a break, so he stepped away from the chapter for a while to eat dinner and brag to his wife about the chapter's completion.

However, after dinner, some of the initial pride had worn off, and he was back to worrying. As he scrolled through the document with fresh eyes, John wondered once again if this would be enough. As fast as the thought came, he pushed it away. There was no use being negative before he even tried.

Drained but determined, he finished up the revisions and attached the final draft to a brief email to Rebecca. He hesitated with his cursor over the send button. With a deep breath, he clicked his mouse. There was no going back now.

John spent the remainder of the weekend periodically checking his email for a reply. He didn't fully expect a response until at least Monday, but that didn't stop him from jumping at every buzz on his phone.

"You're going to give yourself an ulcer if you stay so wound up," Margaret said to him.

John couldn't help it though; he was as excited as he was terrified. Excited to move forward to the next step, and terrified to hear what Rebecca thought of his work.

The email finally came Tuesday morning. John's phone buzzed at breakfast, and when he whipped it out, an email notification labeled "Rebecca Collins" stretched across his screen.

His stomach lurched. Too nervous to tell Margaret, he quickly shoveled the last of his eggs into his mouth and put the plate in the sink, from there slipping back to his office where he could be alone.

He sat down in his office chair and opened the email quickly before he could second guess himself.

John Larsen,

Thank you for sending me the first chapter of your manuscript. Undoubtedly, you have a lot of experience in your field, and this is a great book idea. Unfortunately, your work is not what I am looking for at this time. However, I wish you all the best in your publishing journey and invite you to reach out again when you have more writing experience.

All the best,
Rebecca Collins

John's heart sank.

For a moment he sat frozen, reading the words over and over as if going over them enough times would reveal some mistake or alternate meaning. Instead, the words only began to sound sharper, even the invitation at the end of the letter didn't sound sincere.

"When you have more writing experience."

Did that mean she had an issue with the quality of his writing? Had it really been so bad? He'd tried hard to write what he thought she wanted to read, and he'd spent a long time outlining and perfecting his work. He'd hoped she'd at least see the potential behind the idea, enough to be patient with him as he stumbled through this first draft.

He sank further into his seat. He failed. He'd been given this chance and…he *failed*.

Perhaps Richard had been right all those weeks ago when he told John he didn't recommend he try publishing. He'd been too idealistic to think that he could actually pull something like this off.

Afterall, John was a businessman. He was *not* a writer.

CHAPTER FOUR

The Truth About Book Publishing

When John stepped out of the office, Margaret was waiting for him, her expression questioning.

"I got rejected," John said.

"Oh, honey," Margaret said, stepping in to hug him. "I'm sorry. I know how much work you put into that chapter. Did she at least offer you any feedback?"

John shook his head into her shoulder. "Just to get more experience. I think she could tell I was an amateur. My writing must not be good enough."

Margaret stepped back. "I doubt that very much."

"You don't need to say that, Maggie; I know that chapter was a mess. I wasn't confident in it from the moment I wrote it."

"So, rewrite it," Margaret said firmly. "No one said you only get one chance. It's ok to be upset now, but if you think it can be better, next time, make it better."

"But I can't write," John said, an exasperated tone slipping into his voice. He wasn't really upset with her as much as he was with himself. He wanted to keep trying, but that didn't change the fact that he wasn't qualified.

Margaret put her hands on her hips. "Just because you've never written a book, doesn't mean you can't write. I've read your writing. You may be more used to talking to people face to face, but you're still a great communicator."

"But Rebecca—"

"Is one person. And she may be a professional but that doesn't mean her word is law. Authors get rejected every day, but that doesn't mean they should stop writing. And even if she was right, and your work wasn't good enough, maybe you don't need an agent right now. Maybe you just need some help knowing how to get started."

As soon as Margaret said it, John remembered the card he'd received from Mitch, still sitting at the bottom of his conference bag. He rushed back into the office, looking around until he found the plastic bag against the side of his desk. He dug out the schedule, map, and unused coupons before coming across a handful of business cards he'd collected throughout the day. He sorted through the stack until he came to Mitch's. He hadn't looked closely at it that day, but it had a picture of Mitch in the left side corner, along with an email, phone number, and a line of text at the bottom that read: "Want to write a book? Get a free consultation" followed by a website URL.

John strode back into the hall and showed the card to Margaret. "Remember that writing coach that I told you about? He said he helps authors reach their goals. I suppose I could reach out to him and see what he thinks of the book." He thought about Rebecca's email and cringed. "Then again, I might be a waste of his time if he's used to working with experienced authors."

"His card advertises a free consultation," Maragaret said. "I'm sure he's seen all types of writers. You should do it."

That last bit of encouragement was all John needed.

"Alright, I'll check out his website now." He kissed Maragaret's cheek before turning back into his office. "Thanks, hon."

John sat down at his desk and slowly copied the URL from the card into his web browser. He clicked enter, and the link took him to a simple web page with the same cheery picture of Mitch from his card, and a brief explanation of who he was and what he did. John scrolled down the page to a section marked "Get a Consultation". Below was a basic form and a calendar. John filled in his name, email, phone number, and a summary of his book idea, then he selected a time on the calendar for the next morning.

He was a little nervous to get more feedback so soon after the rejection, but he couldn't help but feel a little closer to his goal.

"Hello, John," Mitch said, smiling wide as John entered the Zoom call. "How are you today?"

"I'm doing well," John said. "I appreciate you being willing to meet with me."

"Of course! There's nothing I like better than meeting new authors.   From what I read in your description; you want to write a book about your experience in business. Looks like you already completed one of the hardest steps: finding something your passionate enough about that you want to write about it."

John chuckled. "I wouldn't say that's the hardest part."

"Well, you'd be surprised. Many people want to write, but it can be tricky for them to figure out what they really want to talk about. Already having a clear direction is a great start. Have you started writing the book already?"

"I have," John grimaced. "I attended the writing conference you spoke at a few weeks ago, and I met an agent who needed a writing sample before she could represent me. I wrote a first chapter to show her…but I don't think it was very good because she decided against being my agent."

John expected Mitch to recoil at the revelation, or at least his expression to turn more hesitant, but the coach looked unfazed. "Publishing is a competitive industry and being rejected by agents or publishers isn't a unique experience. Don't let your first rejection get you down. With some hard work, I'm certain you'll find another agent who likes your work if that's what you wish. But you don't *need* an agent to publish."

John blinked. "I don't?"

"No, many people publish without agents."

"You mean they self-publish."

"That too," Mitch said, "but people traditionally publish without agents too."

John let that sink in a moment. "But someone told me that it is impossible to publish a book without an agent."

"Well, that may have been true a couple decades ago," Mitch said. "And it still is true for specific companies. But the publishing industry has changed a lot from the way it used to be."

John felt like a load had been lifted off him. He hadn't realized how much the stress of finding an agent on top of the stress of finding a publishing company had been weighing on him. He felt much more confident representing himself. Afterall, he'd done pretty well thus far in his life.

"So, you have a first chapter" Mitch said. "Have you written anything else?"

"I've also written an outline."

John felt his face crease into a frown. Just thinking about that document made John's stomach knot. It only overwhelmed him and served to remind him how unsure he was about how the book should be structured.

"I don't like how it turned out though. And I had a hard time following it."

Mitch nodded. "Outlining is a great tool. I often recommend that authors make a list of the key points in their books. However, outlining isn't for everyone; some people do better as pantsers."

Something about that term sounded familiar. H e thought it had been mentioned at one of the panels in the conference. He'd glossed over it at the time because he hadn't heard of it before.

"What's a pantser?" he asked.

"A pantser is someone who doesn't write using an outline. They prefer to start writing and see where their story or idea takes them. When I've worked with pantsers they've told me that having an outline makes them feel like their creativity is boxed in. They also might not know how they want to write their book until they try writing it first. Whereas planners have a hard time knowing where they want to take their story unless they have an outline written ahead of time.

Neither is better than the others, different methods simply work better for different people."

John remembered how frustrating the outlining process had been. He assumed that outlining was something that you *had* to do.

"I think I'm a pantser," John said.

"That's a good thing to know about yourself. I think it's still good you tried outlining so that you know for sure it doesn't work for you, and it helped you brainstorm. Now you have written out everything you want to include in your book. If it works for you, you can keep brain dumping your ideas there when you don't want to forget them. You don't have to include everything you write into the final book either."

Some of what Mitch was saying to him now was reminiscent of the tips he had taught at the writing conference. John needed to go back and reread his notes. He had forgotten about brain dumping when he was writing his first chapter. In fact, he'd forgotten a lot of things. Most importantly, "knowing his reader."

When John wrote that chapter, he hadn't been writing to his intended audience at all. He had been writing what he thought *Rebecca* wanted to hear; he'd been worried about sounding smart, professional, and knowledgeable about writing. He hadn't written what he really wanted to say to other business leaders.

"Why don't you tell me more about your book and your goals for publishing."

John spent the next few minutes explaining his background as an entrepreneur and his goal to help other business leaders find success by sharing the many things he'd learned throughout his career. Rather than hiding his inexperience with writing, John decided to be honest with Mitch, and let him know that this was his first book, and he was a bit intimidated by the whole thing.

When he was finished, Mitch said, "What do you think has been the hardest part about writing so far?"

John thought about that for a moment. "I struggle to be confident in my own writing," he said finally. "I am excited to write this book, but I don't have a lot of experience. I'm worried that I'm not a real writer. I don't know all the grammar or spelling rules or how my book should be formatted. When I was writing the first chapter I couldn't tell if the writing flowed well or not. I don't even know how to publish it once I'm finished. Since I'm so unfamiliar with it all, sometimes I feel frozen."

Mitch listened to him quietly, nodding along here and there. "I want you to know that you are a writer already. There is no finish line you have to pass to call yourself a writer. The moment you decided that you wanted to write a book, you became part of the book business, and you have as much right to publish a book as any other person. Next, I want to talk to you about something that you might remember from my class. Writing is a team sport. Publishing is a team sport."

John gave a small nod. This had been one of the publishing tips.

"Many writers think they have to do this all on their own. But your real job is to just be a **storyteller**. You get the idea onto the page then other people can do the rest. If you don't know if the grammar is right or if the book is flowing well, an editor will. If you don't know how to make a book cover or format the inside of your book, that is what a designer is for. If you don't know how to get your book seen, that is what a marketing team is for. You aren't supposed to do it all on your own, John."

John remembered Richard's snarky comments. "What if my publisher doesn't offer to be a team?"

"That's the thing about being the storyteller," Mitch grinned. "*You* decide where your book goes. We can research what publisher would be the best fit for you. Even if you don't find a publisher that offers every one of these things, you can hire editors, designers, and marketers."

John was quiet for a moment. A bigger question rolled around his mind.

"Be honest with me, Mitch," John said. "Do you really think that I can write this book? You haven't even seen my writing yet."

"I don't need to," Mitch said. He didn't sound like someone trying to make a sale or spare his feelings; he sounded sincere. "I believe anyone can write a book if they really want to. That doesn't mean it's going to be easy. Creating a book that has the quality to be published takes a lot of time and work, but it's very possible. As a writing coach, I'm here to help you. I want to guide you through the process, answer your questions about publishing, and make you a better writer."

Some of John's original excitement came rushing back to him. For the first time since he resolved to write this book, he felt like this was possible.

"Thank you," John said. "If it's alright with you, I would like continue working with you."

"Of course," Mitch said. "Why don't we set up another time for next week? You can go into my calendar and choose a time that works best for you. In the meantime, why don't you send me that first chapter so I can look it over. Or if you like, you can rewrite it and send me the newer version."

John chuckled nervously. "I'm not sure if I can rewrite the first chapter. It was hard enough writing it the first time."

The warmth of Mitch's smile seemed to seep through the computer screen. John didn't know how a person could be so consistently positive.

"Just write. Don't worry about how good it is. Write and see where the story takes you."

CHAPTER FIVE

What Makes a GREAT Book

Writing was much easier when John wasn't trying to be perfect. Sometimes he still struggled to find the right words or to feel like a good writer, but with Mitch's encouragement to "just write" and the comfort that he could always go back later to clean it up, he finished his first chapter pretty quickly. He even had the motivation to complete a second chapter before sending both to Mitch.

"This is great progress," Mitch said the next time they met.

"It doesn't feel too wordy?" John asked.

"There are a few places that could probably be simplified but that isn't for you to worry about right now. Your message is clear, that is what's most important right now."

John nodded. He could accept that. He hadn't expected to be a writing prodigy who never needed to practice. The more he wrote, the faster he would improve.

"You have a great start, John," Mitch continued, "but before we continue further, I want to ask you something."

"Alright."

"What are your publishing goals?"

John furrowed his brow. Hadn't they already gone over this in their first meeting. Maybe Mitch had forgotten, after all, he probably worked with a lot of clients. "Well, I want to share the secrets to success with other—"

"No," Mitch stopped him. "I know the goal of your book, but what are your sales goals?"

John hadn't been expecting a question so business oriented. "The way I always imagined publishing was that the author wrote a good book and threw it over the fence to the publisher then the publisher took charge of the sales portion and threw back bags of money." He replied with a smirk.

Mitch chuckled. "Well, a company that is willing to be a partner to you will help you market. However, authors are still expected to be involved in marketing their own books."

Typically, John would like to sell as many books as he could, but would it sound conceited to say that? Besides, it wasn't like he was trying to make a living off writing.

"I really only care about spreading my message," John said, "so I suppose it doesn't matter how many books I sell."

"I don't think that's really true, John." John was a bit taken aback but Mitch softened the statement with a smile. "Perhaps you don't care about how much money you make by selling books, but if you care about getting your message out there, then you should care about how many books you are selling. Book publishing is only effective when there are book sales, and if no one is buying your book, no one is getting your message."

"You're right," John said. "I do want my book to reach as many people as possible. But I've only finished two chapters, shouldn't I be worrying about this once the book is finished?"

Mitch steepled his fingers together. "In part, yes, but I want to teach you a publishing concept that you can apply both during and after writing that will help you set up your book for successful sales. I call it 'the three-legged stool.'"

John pulled out a pen and paper and readied to take notes.

"Imagine a three-legged stool," Mitch said. "Balance is distributed between each leg to keep it upright. If even one leg is taken out, the stool will topple. Similarly, there are three important things a book must have to sell well. The first is life-changing content, the second is world-changing front and back matter, and the third is effective marketing that results in your readers buying books. Let's delve into each of those categories."

John wrote each category down as a numbered list, leaving ample space between each number to take notes.

"First, let's talk about content. Did you know that 57% of readers put a book down and never pick it up again?" Mitch said. "The content of your book should engage the readers enough that they don't want to put the book down. One of the best ways to do this is to create a story arc. When you instill imagination in your readers, they are more likely to stay with you. What do you know about story arcs, John?"

"A story arc is the bare bones of the story, isn't it? It's what makes a story a story."

"Right, story arcs have been used in writing for forever. You may not have noticed it, but almost every story follows the same beats of storytelling. Imagine you're watching a movie. What happens in the first ten minutes?"

"You meet the main character," John said.

"Exactly! You get to know who they are, and you see their every day situation. But then something happens. It may be tragic, exciting, or fun, but whatever it is, it takes the character out of their every day normal. The story builds on that something until the character reaches a crisis or a celebration that seems impossible. That is the climax. What quickly follows is what I like to call redemption for the character. As the story concludes, the character has changed from the person they were at the start. Does this pattern sound familiar?"

"Yes." John could already think of a dozen movies that followed the same model.

"That's because story arcs are used in every best selling book or movie out there."

"Isn't a story arc usually used for fiction books, though?" John said. "Something like that doesn't apply to the type of book I'm writing."

"That's a fair point. Not every book follows a story arc. But let me ask you this. What is the last great book you've read?"

John thought a moment. He'd recently been getting into Agatha Christie; he liked the excitement and twists that came with a good mystery. "Murder on the Orient Express."

"Alright, what's the last great textbook you've read."

John's mind blanked. Had he even bought a textbook since college? He sometimes bought informational books that looked interesting, but for the life of him, he couldn't think of a single title, or what the books had been about.

After a few seconds, Mitch broke the silence. "You remember the book way better, right? That's because one is a story, and the other is simply a transfer of information. People tend to remember information they get from a story more than information that is rambled off to them. That's why I like to put story arcs in nonfiction work. Because if you want readers to stay engaged and to remember your message, telling a story is a great way to make sure the information sticks. That may take the form of a fictional narrative or in the form of creative non-fiction."

It was like Mitch turned on a switch in John's head. His book began by introducing himself and then shifted to how he first began in business and how he started to learn the things that led to his success. Subconsciously, he had already begun writing a story. Maybe it wasn't exactly like the action books he liked to read, but a story, nonetheless. A story where he was the main character, learning and failing until he reached where he was now.

"Let's say you're writing 3000-word chapters, a good ratio would be 2000 words of story and 1000 words of what you want your readers to learn. That way you engage your readers imagination while enforcing information."

John made note of that, but another thought came to him. "I noticed this when I first started writing, but why do authors and publishers measure length in words instead of pages? I feel like using pages is easier."

"Ah, yes. A lot of new writers are curious about this because that's how you measure the length of a book as a reader. However, pages aren't a reliable source of measurement when you're a writer. They depend on the dimensions of the book, the size of the font, the type of paper you use, and things like that. Meanwhile, the number of words isn't going to change. A good rule of thumb is to write chapters around 3,000 to 4,500 words long. That gives room for editors to work it down later. A whole book is typically 20,000 to 60,000 words. There is no hard rule to this though. It's more important to get the reader to stay with you than to ramble trying to reach a certain word count. Just take the time to write a great engaging story. And like I've told you before, don't worry about being perfect. When you're first writing a book, you just need to get the story out. It will go through plenty of edits before it is done."

Mitch waited a few moments as John finished writing notes then asked, "Any questions so far?"

John was pretty solid on the information he was sharing in his book, but one of the bigger challenges was making it engaging with some form of story.

"Do you have any tips when it comes to storytelling?" he asked.

"Oh, *lots,* but for the sake of time, I'll limit myself to just a couple. We've talked about planners and pantsers, but a simple tool that both groups can use is a mind map. You can look up mind map tools online, but basically, they are a series of circles and squares where you can write topics and plot points. One of the nice things about them is that you can move the pieces around. That way, if you aren't sure what order you want things to go, you can easily reorganize them.

"The second thing I like to do is create character biographies. Whether they're real or fictional, I try to get to know the people I'm writing about. Some of the things I might write about are their family, their hobbies, their favorite sports team. As I get to know my characters, they begin to feel more real, and it's easier to write them. Also, if you ever forget a detail about a character, it's nice to have a bio to look back on to see what you originally said. Does all of that make sense?"

John made up a note to look up a mind mapping tool later. It sounded less restrictive than the outline. "Yes, that helps."

"Great! Let's move on to the next leg of the stool: front and back matter. I think a lot of people focus so much on the content that they overlook how critical this part of the book is. The front matter is everything from the cover until chapter one. This includes, the dedication, table of contents, acknowledgements, forward, introduction, or anything else that may be needed before the story begins. Whereas the back matter is everything from the last word to the back cover. This might be the author bio or an author's note."

"I feel a little bad saying this," John said, "but usually I skip a lot of that stuff to get to the story. Is it really that important to selling a book?"

Mitch nodded. "Each of these items has a particular task, and I think you use them a lot more than you think. For example, the cover's job is to catch your attention. Once you've picked it up, you probably open it up and read the book description (blurb) that tells you what the book is about. From there, you might turn the book over and read the endorsements on the back cover. If you were curious about the book's content, you could flip to the table of contents and get a good idea of each chapter's topic. Also, let's say you decide to buy the book and read it all the way to the end. The back matter may lead you to a website, a course, or other instructions the author has left to keep you engaged in his message."

Mitch was right; John *had* done all those things. Maybe he'd been taking front and back matter for granted. Since all books had that content, he'd thought that was just how books were. He hadn't realized just how intentional each of those pieces were to making books sales. He probably wouldn't have bought any of the books he owned if he hadn't been able to look at a blurb or endorsements. Not to mention all the books he had been led to by reading author bios.

"I didn't realize how much business is involved in publishing books," he said.

Mitch nodded. "When people think about publishing, a lot of people focus on the writing portion, and they forget that they need a lot more than good writing to sell books. That brings us to the last leg of the stool: marketing. I'll be honest with you, most book publishers don't do marketing, not even traditional publishers. These days, a lot of traditional publishers like to see how popular you are, so that you can sell your book with already existing fame. That's why it's important to find a publishing company that has a marketing team for their authors, hire a marketing team, or familiarize yourself with marketing methods to do it yourself. Whatever your choice, you need to be willing to be involved in the marketing of your books because marketing is crucial to making sales."

John didn't need an explanation for that part. Throughout his career, he'd become very familiar with the link between marketing and a business's success. If pictured marketing his book the way he marketed his past businesses, it didn't feel quite so unfamiliar. Still, with his inexperience, he should make sure he wasn't missing any information.

"I've overseen a lot of marketing in my career," John said. "How different is marketing books?"

Mitch tilted his head thoughtfully. "There are a couple uniquenesses, but I wouldn't say it's very different. What are some methods your familiar with?"

"Social media," John said immediately. "Everyone is on some platform or another. It was always one of the strongest ways to advertise or get information out about my business-es."

"Yes," Mitch said, pointing at John through the screen. "Social media is a key tool. One of the challenges that comes with social media marketing is that it is always changing. Platforms rise and fall in popularity; trends change every week; it can be hard for authors to keep up. However, if you have a good publisher, they will have people to stay on top of that for you. What other methods are you familiar with?"

"Public relations. I always made sure that my businesses had a good public image. We did that through interviews and organizing events to advertise the product."

"Are you comfortable speaking in front of people?"

"Oh, yes. I think part of why I've struggled with this is book is because I communicate better verbally than I do through writing."

"That's good," Mitch said. "A lot of authors get nervous speaking in public, but public relations are required in this business to build credibility. I always encourage authors to get training and practice so that they can feel comfortable enough to speak in interviews, podcasts, or other media.

"And public relations are directly linked to another im-portant marketing strategy, which is to take advantage of first-person marketing opportunities. That is, things like book signings or interviews for articles or tv. It's very important that you, the author, make connections and relationships with your readers. You represent your book and your message. If you alienate your audience, they won't buy your next book." He paused a moment, waiting for questions or comments. When John stayed quiet, he said, "Anything else?"

John idly tapped his pen against the page. "Off the top of my head, the only other thing I can think of is customer service. When we built a good reputation with customers, they were more likely to recommend our business to their friends and family."

"Yes, depending on how you decide to publish your book, you'll have more or less responsibility in this manner, but it's still a great thing to be aware of."

"What do you mean by that?"

"Well, if you ever decided to self-publish a book, you are in charge of your own distribution and sales. If you go out of town and someone orders a book, you'll have to send it to them late. If enough people get upset, giving you lows stars and reviews, it can kill your reputation. My number one rule when it comes to customer complaints is to just give them a refund. Even if they're in the wrong, let them keep the book and refund them their money. You don't want them to leave negative reviews on your book, and who knows, if you are understanding towards them, it may lead to a positive review. But ultimately, I recommend having a separate person manage emails, questions, and distribution. That way it isn't all dependent on you. If you have a publisher, they would be the ones in the charge of that."

John nodded along to Mitch's suggestions. In his business, he'd always tried to ensure his customers had positive experiences. They were much more likely to be lenient to mistakes or leave good feedback when they felt the business cared about them.

"Well," Mitch said, "you've already named most of my marketing strategies, but there are a couple more items I'd like to share with you."

"Alright." John readied his pen once again.

"An important key to a successful book is endorsements and recommendations. When you first release your book, endorsements are even more important than sales. You can build those endorsements into your campaign, which will lead to more book sales later. I told you earlier that endorsements were an important part of a book's back matter. Readers like to know other's opinions on a book and having that recommendation can be the push needed for someone to buy the book rather than put it back on the shelf."

"How do I get someone to endorse my book?"

"Write a great one," Mitch said

John blinked.

Mitch laughed. "I know that sounds easier said than done, but it's true. If you put in the work to write a great book, you're not going to have trouble asking people for endorsements. There are companies out there who will pay people for endorsements or leave a lot of good reviews, but if you want to do it right, put your effort into making your book the best it can be."

Mitch glanced down at the bottom corner of the screen. "Ah, it looks like our time is almost up, but let me leave you with one last piece of advice. When possible, capture demographic data up front. Unfortunately, the online stores and brick and mortar book shops don't collect that sort of data. However, this data is so helpful when you are marketing your second book. It will help you know what sort of audience is most interested in your writing, so your marketing can be more targeted. There are some publishing companies who offer to collect that data for you, or if you self-publish, you can request that information as you distribute your book."

"That makes sense," John said.

"That's the three-legged stool method. Content, front and back matter, and marketing. Keep those three things in mind and you'll be on your way to success."

"Thank you, Mitch. I really appreciate you helping me with these things."

"Of course, that's what I do. Why don't you get started on chapter three, and we can set up another appointment to discuss how you feel the book is going once you're finished. Of course, you can write more than one chapter if you get on a roll."

"Sounds good," John said. "Thanks again."

After John ended the Zoom call, he pulled up his document. The conversation had left him excited to continue writing. If he kept up like this, he might be finished with the book within a couple of months.

A thrill ran through him as he pictured his book in stores and on bookshelves. He shouldn't get ahead of himself, but he couldn't wait to begin submitting to publishers.

CHAPTER SIX

Publishing, Publishing, and More Publishing

John picked up a carton of strawberries from the produce section and placed it in his shopping cart. He pulled out his phone to check over the grocery list Margaret had sent him. He still needed milk and chicken breasts. He turned the cart around and started toward the poultry section.

Over the last few weeks, he'd spent a lot of time writing and rewriting his book. After going over the chapters with Mitch, he felt *so* close to being ready to publish. But maybe he'd been a little obsessed lately because Margaret had sent him to the grocery store with instructions to "get his mind on something else for a while."

He walked slowly along the refrigerated wall. Chicken thighs, chicken tenders, chicken wings… Ah! Chicken breasts.

"Oh, hey!"

John stopped, hand half closed around the package, and looked up. A young woman with a bright red bob and a Pride and Prejudice t-shirt stood in front of him, a handheld shopping basket looped over the crook of her arm. Had he seen her somewhere before?

"You were at the university writing conference a while ago, right?"

John quickly sifted through his head for all the people he had met at the conference. She wasn't one of the agents. Maybe one of the panelists? It suddenly struck him.

Oh. She was one of the authors from the bookselling area.

"Yes," he said, pointing at her tentatively, "and you write fantasy books?"

"That's right. Or as I call it, romantasy. I'm Betty by the way, I'm not sure if I ever really introduced myself."

"John," John said, shaking hands with her. She was a lot easier to talk to when she wasn't trying to sell him something,

"Do you write too? I think I remember you asking about publishing."

John nodded. "I'm writing a book on business. I'm getting ready to submit my manuscript to a few places soon."

"That's great! Business is not my thing, but I know there's a big audience for non-fiction. So, you're thinking you'll go the traditional publishing route?"

"Oh, yeah," John said. How did he go about explaining that without offending her. From the way Richard had talked about self-publishing, it almost felt like a cop out from 'real' publishing. And from what little he'd heard at the conference; it sounded harder to make sales. He tried for a diplomatic response. "I'm just not sure if self-publishing would be right for me."

Betty nodded. "Self-publishing isn't for everyone. I think it gets a bad rap because anyone can do it, but when done right, it really is a great publishing option. That being said, it's *a lot* of work."

"Really?"

"*Oh,* yeah." Betty began listing responsibilities off on her fingers. "You're in charge of all your own shipping and returns. You have to do all your own marketing. You need to organize your own speaking engagements. You have to organize your own book signings, and if you've never done one before, let me tell you, it's a lot harder to set up than it seems. Especially if no one knows who you are yet. Not to mention the self-publishing book market is really saturated because of how easy it is to do. It's pretty easy for your book to get buried in all the other books being published, and since so much of it is low quality, it's hard to get readers to trust that your book is good. Overall, you need to be really driven because you are your own publishing company. It's great to not have to worry about an agent or the approval of a company, but you have to wear a lot of hats."

"What made you decide to self-publish?" John asked.

"Honestly, I write more for fun than for profit, and I didn't want to go through the whole submission and rejection thing. I just like knowing people are out there reading my work. So, for what I wanted out of my books, publishing on Amazon was perfect. They have me labeled as a bestseller and enough bragging rights for me. I promote my books on social media, and I go to conferences here and there, but I don't stress too much about numbers. If I was trying to make a career out of writing or wanting to sell thousands of books, I imagine I'd have to do a lot more."

"But it is possible for someone to have good sales as a self-published author?" John asked.

"Yeah, I've seen a lot of successful self-published authors. Most of those people already had a big fanbase when they published though. Or they're really diligent about marketing their book and making sure it's seen. Like I said, it's a lot of work, and it's not for everyone."

That made a lot of sense. If a celebrity were to self-publish a book, of course their book would do well. He could also see how someone dedicated to making writing books their career could do well if they treated it like a business. He didn't know nearly enough about the ins and outs of publishing to feel confident doing that though. He also didn't really want to make writing his career. Traditional publishing still seemed like the best option for him.

Something Betty said stuck out to him though.

"Sorry, if this sounds blunt," he said, "but you said you're an Amazon bestseller. How does that work if you aren't selling thousands of books?"

Betty's face warmed a bit. "Oh yeah," she said, chuckling nervously. "Being a bestseller on Amazon isn't as impressive as it sounds. It makes a great selling point, and I am proud of it, but Amazon will mark something a best seller based on how well it sells compared to other books in a category. For example, I like to include knitting in my stories, so the books get marked under the knitting category, even though they aren't really about that. But because it sells more than the other books about knitting, it gets marked as a bestseller."

"I see," John said. That didn't sound very fair.

"I didn't do that on purpose though," Betty said quickly - She lied. "I put in a few categories and from there Amazon placed in other places that seemed relevant based on keywords and topic. And I'm also a bestseller in the witches and wizards subcategory which I'll admit is a little niche, but still."

"No, no, I'm not judging you," John said. It wasn't how he wanted to go about things, but if it wasn't purposefully dishonest (it was), he didn't see anything wrong with using whatever rankings were awarded to a writer. Even if just for one's own validation. "I was just curious. I think it's great that you've been able to reach that rank. And thank you for explaining this all to me. I didn't know much about self-publishing."

Betty's confident smile returned. "Of course! It's always nice to talk to a fellow writer. Good luck with publishing your book."

John thanked her, and after grabbing their respective groceries, they parted ways. As he wandered toward the back of the store for the milk, his mind replayed pieces of the conversation. Even though he'd learn some new things, he also had more questions now.

If the Amazon bestseller list wasn't always reliable, what did that mean about all the other bestseller lists out there? Also, what information was he still missing about publishing options? It seemed every time he thought he understood publishing he found out about something new. He felt like a fish who just realized the body of water he was swimming in was a piece of the ocean.

Oh well, he thought as he placed the milk jug into his cart. *There's no use stressing. I just need to keep learning.*

He chuckled to himself as he checked out a few minutes later. He hadn't gotten his mind off book writing after all.

"I have some questions about publishing," John said in his next zoom meeting with Mitch.

Mitch looked a little surprised. The last few meetings had been all about perfecting John's writing, so he probably hadn't been expecting the new topic. Even so, he said, "Of course, what were you wanting to know?"

"I was talking to someone recently about publishing, and I realized I don't know much about all the available publishing options."

Mitch ran his fingers through his mustache thoughtfully. "You're right. Since you've been leaning toward traditional publishing, I hadn't thought to tell you about other options. Like I told you in the past, the publishing world has changed a lot. It used to be that there were a few great book publishers. They were very selective, so it was difficult to get published. As it evolved, you had to get an agent to pitch your book to publishers, then people started publishing their own books, and now the world of publishing is wide open. Why don't we start by talking about traditional publishing since that's what your most interested in?"

"Alright," John agreed.

Mitch rubbed his mustache for a few more seconds, as if deciding where to begin. "In traditional publishing, there are about 8 big publishers," he finally said. "Then there are a bunch of smaller companies. Typically, you approach traditional publishers, especially the big ones, with an agent, but as I've told you when we met, agents are no longer necessary for every company. The pros of traditional publishing are that you will have a team to help you and that they will make sure that your content is all there. The con is that it is more difficult to get into."

John raised his hand slightly to interject. "But if someone was to be accepted into a traditional publishing company, they sometimes get an advance, right? That would be a pro too."

"Ah, the myth of the advance," Mitch said. "The truth is, unless you have the potential to sell millions of books—that's more likely to happen if you're already popular—you're not going to get an advance. An advance is simply an advance on the royalties you are expected to make. If a company can't guarantee they're going to get that money back, they're not going to want to give you an advance. These days most authors are not offered an advance, so I wouldn't bank on that when going the traditional route."

"How many books would you say traditional publishers sell?"

Mitch blew out a longer breath. "This may sound discouraging, but most published authors don't sell more than 500 books. But like any business, as you know, it takes a lot of time and investment and grit to be successful."

"Huh," John said with a nervous laugh. "I'm a bit more intimidated now."

"That's ok," Mitch said also chuckling. "Traditional publishing is speculative. It's a gamble. You don't know for sure if you'll be accepted. But if you put everything you can into your book, you should give it a try. It's not an impossible feat. If I could tell authors only one thing, it would be to not be discouraged by rejection."

That seemed easier said than done, but John decided not worry about something that hadn't happened yet. Like Mitch said, it was difficult not impossible, and he'd been painstakingly working on his book for a while now.

"The next big type of publishing is self-publishing."

"Oh," John interrupted. "I ran into a self-published author the other day. She told me a lot about the pros and cons."

"Good," Mitch said. "Talking to people with experience in the matter is one of the best ways to gain information. I'll just tell you a few basics then. In the past, people who self-published would slap together books themselves, find somewhere to print a bunch of copies, and then try to go out and sell them. The self-publishing we know today sprang mostly from Amazon when they created e-reader. They needed content, so they created a way for people to self-publish ebooks. The ebook space alone has 5 million titles. Unfortunately, because it's so simple, the market has been flooded with marginal work and very few of them sell as many as 500 books. While self-publishing is the right thing for some people, many people are not equipped to do all the work required to be successful. Another con is that the media isn't as interested in self-published books. When something is traditionally published people assume it has been vetted already, but when a book is self-published people don't take it as seriously. Even if your book is great because of the stereotypes surrounding self-publishing, people may doubt whether your book is good quality. For these reasons, the media often won't do stories on self-published works."

John nodded along as Mitch spoke. That added up with what Betty had told him.

"The third type of publishing is hybrid publishing," Mitch continued. "This isn't much different from self-publishing. The difference is that you give your book to a company, and for a fee, they do the layout and send it to be printed and distributed. They don't care what the contents of your book are as long as you pay them to put it together. This can be very effective, and the price ranges anywhere between very inexpensive to around $50,000. However, hybrid publishers usually don't market your book. Even if they say they will, that usually just means that they create ads for your book; they're not creating an effective marketing campaign for you. Hybrid publishing isn't bad, just know that all they're really doing is printing it. Making a physical books for you. After that, you are the one who has to make sure it gets sold."

"How do authors usually decided what would be best for them?" From the sound of it, there were a lot of pros and cons to every option.

"A couple of things you need to think about when deciding on a method of publishing are risk and revenue."

"Risk?"

"When I say risk, I mean how much money and time you're willing to spend to put your book together. You could spend a little money to try publishing yourself and learn from the process. You could pay a hybrid publisher to put your book together. You could pay a ghostwriter to write for you. You could go to a traditional publisher and work hard to get accepted. As long as your comfortable with the risks you're taking, there's no wrong way to do it."

"That's similar to one of my business principles 'count your costs.' When starting a business, you have to decide what your willing to give to make it thrive. It's the same with publishing, but whatever route you take will decide how much of that money and time you have to put in."

"Exactly," Mitch said. "You do everything your willing to do, and you hope it will come back to you. It may sound a little uncertain, but anything new is."

"And the differences in revenue?" John said.

"Well, if you go with traditional publishing, you get about 2%-5% royalty of your book, depending on the company. Self-publishing or hybrid publishing will get you nearly all the revenue, but again, that dependent on you selling your own books. I also warn you that when hybrid publishers offer almost all your royalties, it means they don't plan on doing much, if any, marketing. Because if they're not taking any royalties, where are they getting the money to create a marketing campaign? Basically, if it seems too good to be true, it probably is."

John mulled over it all for a moment. He was glad for the new information, but after hearing it all, his opinion hadn't changed much.

"I know that I could market and sell my own book," John said. "I have the grit and business experience to do it. But I never intended this book to be something that takes up all my time. Because of that, I still think traditional publishing is my preferred option."

"It's always good to know your options," Mitch said. "Even if to confirm that you're on the right path. Did you have any other questions?"

John thought back to what Betty said about being an Amazon bestseller. He wondered about the big best seller lists like the New York Times. When so many people used those lists to find good books, surely, they were trustworthy. Still, he was curious.

"Well, I was wondering a bit about the bestseller lists. I've always thought making that list was huge deal, but I've heard some things lately that have made me question that."

"Making the best seller's list isn't as simple as selling more books than other people. For one, there is an editorial influence over each best seller model, and you have to be approved by their editorial board. If you write a conservative book, they won't rate you at New York times but they will at Wall Street Journal and vice versa. They also record how many books are being sold by the barcode, and since tons of books are sold online every day, counting it by barcode is not a good representation of a best seller. You also need to think about where that ranking is coming from. Publisher's Weekly can give you an accurate list, but some stores, like Amazon have a lot of niche categories where you may become a best seller from selling 10 books."

"So, making the bestseller's list doesn't mean anything?"

Mitch's eyebrows shot up. "Oh, it's definitely something to be proud of! Even if there are other elements to it, it's still not easy." He grinned. "If you end up making one of those lists, by all means, sing about it from the housetops!"

"I can certainly hope," John said with a laugh.

"Was there any other questions you had?"

"Just my final chapter. I'm not sure if the conclusion is strong enough."

"Well, let me pull it up and remind myself." Mitch clicked his computer mouse a couple times, eyes flicking around the screen as he navigated to the document. "Wow, final chapter already. You've put a lot of work into this over the past few months."

John certainly had. It had been a lot of hard work, but he felt proud of what he had accomplished so far. He could already picture that book up on his shelf. Or on other people's shelves. It wouldn't be long now before he shared his message with the world.

CHAPTER SEVEN

How to Handle Rejection

John finished the book within the week. He'd gone over each chapter with Mitch throughout the writing and revision process, so he felt fairly confident that it was at least good enough to start submitting. If it needed any further work, he hoped that whatever publishing company accepted him had an in-house editor to help.

He started out searching for companies that specialized in non-fiction, but quickly branched out to a few others that had good reviews and published all genres of books. He even submitted to a couple of the big New York companies just for the heck of it.

It turned out that submitting a manuscript had more steps than he had expected. Each company had their own submission guidelines. Some wanted just the first chapter; some wanted the whole manuscript. A few places required a query letter, others a full book summary. Not to mention everything had to be formatted in a particular way. Then there was the fact that many companies only accepted submissions at certain times of the year.

By the time he was done tailoring his submissions to each publishers' needs, he was exhausted. But at least it was done. Now, all he had to do was wait.

Waiting was hard.

John knew that publishers probably received *a lot* of submissions. But with every day that passed, he still couldn't stop wondering what was taking so long. Had anyone even read it yet? Did they like it? Maybe it was taking so long because they liked it so much, they wanted to read the whole thing. Or because it was so bad it wasn't even worth responding to.

He tried to shake the negative thoughts away as soon as they came to him. He shouldn't worry about things he had no control over. He'd already done his part, now it was in the publishers' ball court.

"I'm pretty sure publishing companies don't send emails at 10pm," Margaret teased one evening as his phone screen illuminated their bedroom.

"I know," he said quickly placing the phone face down on his nightstand. "I just can't stop thinking about it."

"It will all work out," She gave him a playful shove. "So stop worrying about it."

Easier said than done.

When the first letter came, about a month had passed. John was working on his computer when the email notication suddenly appeared in the corner of his screen. He clicked it open immediately.

John,

Thank you for sending your manuscript The Blueprint to Success. Your book has a lot of potential, but unfortunately, it is not what we are looking for at this time. We hope that The Blueprint to Success finds a home at another company, and we encourage you to submit to Starlight Books again in the future.

Always keep writing,

Janet Evans
Chief Acquisitions Editor
Starlight Books

John's heart sank. It wasn't the answer he'd been hoping for, but it wasn't wholly unexpected either. He would have been surprised if the first email *had* been an acceptance. At least they seemed to have liked the book, and besides there were plenty of other companies he needed to hear back from.

The next letter came in the next morning.

Dear Mr. Larsen,

We appreciate your patience in this decision-making process, and we thank you for considering us. We regret to inform you that we cannot accept your manuscript for publication. With hundreds of submissions received each year, we can only choose a select few. We hope this does not discourage you from submitting to us again in the future.

All the best,

Franklin Patterson
Acquisitions Editor
Old Mountain Publishing

And then another came in that afternoon.

John Larsen,

Thank you for submitting your manuscript The Blueprint to Success. It's obvious you've put in a lot of work; how-

ever, your manuscript is not a good fit for our company. We wish you all the best in your writing journey, and we hope to read more from you in the future.

Carol Reed
Chief of Acquisitions
Willow Tree Books

Over the week, several more letters piled into John's inbox. Never had the words "unfortunately" or "we regret" or "however" brought him such frustration. And if they all wanted him to submit again so badly, why didn't they accept his manuscript now? Though it was worse when he could tell the letter was a generic rejection sent to everyone. It made him wonder how much time they'd spent even looking at his manuscript.

As the rejections continued to pour in, his expectations lowered and lowered, until when he received an email he flicked his eyes to the middle of the paragraph to get the rejection over with quicker.

"The next one could be a yes," Margaret said everytime his face fell. It was a nice gesture, but John was beginning to doubt if that was true. After all, when facing so many rejections, maybe there was something wrong with the book. Though he couldn't think of what that could be. He knew the book wasn't perfect, but he'd thought it good. Mitch had assured him that it was good.

Perhaps that was the problem. He only had the opinions of himself, Margaret, and Mitch. Maybe it would help to have another set of eyes on it. Someone professional who hadn't been looking at it for months.

John had lived next door to Richard long enough to know he returned home 5pm before heading back to the college for night classes. Around 5:30, John gave him a call.

"Hello?" the professor's voice crackled dryly from the other end.

"Hey, Richard, how are you doing?"

"I'm doing fine. What can I do for you?"

It seemed like the polite way of saying, "Why are you calling me?"

"Well, you see, I finished by book a while ago," John said. "I have submitted my manuscript to several publishers but haven't had any success so far. I was wondering if you'd be willing to take a look at it and give me some pointers? Maybe if I figure out what's wrong and do another revision I'll have better luck."

There was a long pause.

"Sorry, John. I'm too busy with student essays to read anything else right now. Have you tried talking to your agent?"

"Uh, no. I decided not to go that route."

Another long paused. "Well, maybe writing just isn't for you."

The comment struck John almost as hard as a physical blow. All the doubts from the agent's rejection a few months ago came rushing back.

"Maybe," he said quietly. "Thanks anyway, Richard."

He hung up the phone and leaned way back in his office chair, running his hands up his face and into his hair.

He really couldn't do this, could he? He knew he had been told not to be discouraged by rejection but this was ridiculous.

He halfheartedly opened his manuscript document and began scanning through the pages. What could he change? How could he make this better? He'd been so confident in the work a few weeks ago, but now every bit of it seemed mediocre.

Maybe writing isn't for you.

John hit the close button on the document a little harder than he needed to, and the manuscript blipped off the screen. He sighed heavily as he stood up. He should take a break from thinking about this.

That break turned from an evening, to a week, to two weeks. The book still came to his mind, but he did his best to push it to the far back of his brain. He didn't mention it in conversation, changing the subject whenever it was brought up, and he ignored the document while he was on his computer. Thinking about the book only filled him with disappointment. Disappointment in himself, disappointment that he wouldn't get the results he'd daydreamed about. Maybe eventually, somewhere in the future, he'd be able to speak about it with indifference. 'Oh, I tried to write a book once, but it didn't work out.' But for now, maybe it was better to forget he'd tried.

He'd thought he'd been hiding his feelings on the matter pretty well, but one day, while they were in the family room watching a movie, he felt Margaret's eyes on him.

"I think you should talk to Mitch," she said suddenly.

"Why?"

"To find out what you should do next."

"He's already helped me as much as he can," John said. "If I'm not a good enough writer to be published, talking isn't going to change that."

Margaret frowned. "Don't say that, you're a good writer."

John smiled humorlessly. "I think you're a little bit biased."

"I'm serious. You're not being rejected because you're a bad writer, so you should at least ask Mitch for advice. If he tells you there's nothing he can do to help, at least you'll know. At least it would be better than moping around."

John sat up straighter in his seat. "I haven't been moping."

"If you say so. But I still think you should talk to Mitch."

Margaret left it at that.

John tried to ignore the comment and go back to the movie, but for some reason it kept eating at him. That night, he tossed and turned in bed, grappling with whether he should really ask for help or just let it lie. He already felt like a failure, he didn't need Mitch to know their sessions had been a waste of time. He also didn't see any way that the coach could help him. But at the same time, if he did nothing, he might always wonder if he could have done more.

John rolled on his back and stared at the ceiling. He wasn't the type of person to give up without trying everything first. At the very least, it would be good to get closure.

First thing in the morning, he scheduled a meeting with Mitch.

∼∼

When Mitch popped on the screen, bright smile peeking from under his mustache, John wondered why he'd ever thought that the coach would be disappointed in him.

"Hey, John, I haven't heard from you for a while. What are the updates on your book?"

John grimaced. "Well…I've been rejected by every publisher that I've submitted to.

Mitch's smile fell a little. "I'm sorry, John, that's never easy."

"It's fine." John tried to force a chuckle, but it fell flat. "I knew I wasn't much of a writer anyway."

"Hold on," Mitch said, lifting one of his hands like a stop sign. "Rejection doesn't mean you aren't a good writer."

"I know, but when you're rejected as many times as I—"

"Rejection happens to everyone," Mitch interrupted. "You know Steven King?"

John paused a moment. "Of course. I'm not a horror fan, but basically everyone knows Steven King."

"He was rejected by 30 publishers before he published his debut novel. The year it was released it sold over a million copies. I'm sure he felt like giving up at the time, but if he had, he would have missed out on major success."

"Ok, but—"

"J.K. Rowling was rejected by 12 publishers while trying to publish *Harry Potter*. Basically every successful author has faced rejection. It didn't mean they were bad at writing or that their ideas weren't good enough. It just meant it wasn't the right publisher, or the right time, or the right draft. There's any number of reasons for a manuscript to be rejected, but none of them are a good enough reason for you to give up."

John was quiet, letting that sink in. He felt so different compared to those other writers. Like they were real writers, and he was an imposter. But…maybe they felt the same way when they were starting out.

"Rejection is hard," Mitch continued, "but rather than looking at it as a dead end, look at it as a stepping stone. Some writers save their rejection letters. They pin them to the wall or put them in a folder. They show an author's effort. And they may just give the motivation to prove all those publishers wrong."

"But what do I do? I don't even know why they're rejecting my book."

"If you like, you could revise it again. But I've read your book, and I think it's good enough quality for publication, so in my opinion, you should just keep submitting it."

"And if it just keeps being rejected?"

"Then keep trying. You could search out a community writing group to give you more feedback. If you're worried about mistakes, you could hire an editor. If you put out enough effort, something will come back to you. For now, I would just focus on finding more publishers and measure your options as you go."

"Well, I guess being rejected isn't any worse than letting it gather dust in my drafts," John said. "I'll give it another try."

He still felt a little doubtful, but over the next couple of months, John submitted to every relevant publisher he could find. He decided to take Mitch's advice and save the rejection letters he was sent; he imagined them as proof of his hard work rather than proof of failure. It still hurt to receive them, but the more he received, the more accustomed he became, and the less it bothered him.

At a neighborhood get together, Richard asked him if he was still working on the book or if he'd given up.

"Oh, I'm still plugging along," John said.

"If having a book matters that much to you, maybe you should just self-publish to have one on the shelf."

John smiled. "Thanks for the advice, Richard, but I think I'll try it my way a while longer."

One day, his phone buzzed, alerting him of yet another reply from a publisher. He opened the email and automaticcaly began scanning for the usual rejection. He froze. He started the letter again from the beginning.

Hello John,

Thank you for sending your manuscript The Blueprint to Success. We enjoyed reading about your story, and we are happy to inform you that we would like to publish it. We believe that your experiences in business and leadership would be a great fit for our company. Please, let us know if you'd like to accept our offer, and we can set up a meeting to go over the details.

All the best,

Amy Wright
Chief Acquisitions Editor
Everscholar Books

John's heart soared. He was an author.

CHAPTER 8

A New Beginning

John decided to do a little research before accepting the company's publication offer. He had applied to so many companies, he needed a refresher to remember all of the details. It turned out that the company published mostly non-fiction, ranging from memoirs to biographies to self-help books. As he browsed through their recently published works, he recognized a few titles he seen in the store. That had to be a good sign. Their social media pages also seemed positive.

Satisfied that the company was legitimate, John emailed back for more details. Within a couple days, he was attending a Zoom meeting with the acquisitions editor, Amy. She was a curly haired, blonde woman about his age, and her positive tone immediately set him at ease.

"Let me explain a little bit about our publishing plan," Amy said after introductions. "After we acquire a book, we send it to our in-house editors. They'll let you know if you need to make any big changes to the manuscript. If it only needs a copy edit and line edit—that is things like grammar, punctuation, cutting down repetition and wordiness, etc.— then they will mark all the changes that need to be made with a Microsoft tool called 'track changes'. They will then send the manuscript back to you so that you can make those changes. Once the book is in its final draft, we'll put you in contact with one of our designers to make a book cover and format it correctly. From there, we'll start marketing your book for distribution.

"Oh, you provide marketing?" John said. From what Mitch had said, even some of the big traditional publishers didn't do that anymore so that was nice to hear.

"Yes, we still encourage our authors to be a part of the marketing process, but we organize a marketing campaign for all the books we publish."

"How do you go about distribution?" He'd come across a few companies during his research that only published as ebooks or required purchases to made through their own website. Though that didn't seem to be the case here, he didn't want to be overly hasty and have his book published where, even with marketing, it may have trouble being found.

"When we publish a book, we release it in hardcover and paperback first, then we release to ebook, and then audiobook. Our goal is to distribute books to every online and brick and mortar store we can. That includes the big sellers like Amazon and Barnes and Noble."

"That's good to hear. Out of curiosity, if you release books in different forms in stages, why do you start with printed books? Wouldn't it be cheaper to start with ebooks, gather an audience, and print books afterward?"

"That's good logic," Amy said, "but hardcover and paperback books make up about 80% of book sales. Despite the popularity of ebooks several years ago, people still prefer having a physical book they can hold. Not only is turning the pages a familiar feeling, but if someone *really* like a book, they usually want a hardcover copy to keep on their shelf. Meanwhile, ebooks make up about 15% of book sales. People usually buy an ebook because they want to save on money, but unfortunately, they usually don't go back to read it again later. That's why we want to promote your book in print first because that's more likely to reach a wider spread of people."

John did the math in his head. "Does that mean that audiobooks only make up 5% of sales?" Honestly, he was surprised. Most people he talked to these days were listening to audiobooks because they didn't have the time to sit down and read.

Amy nodded. "That's right. The popularity for audiobooks is growing every day, but it still makes up a relatively small portion of sales. One of the problems with audiobooks, especially with with nonfiction books, it that readers aren't fully present while they listen. Think about it, when do you listen an audiobook?"

"When I'm driving or cleaning."

"Right, when you're doing another task. Oftentimes, you are not focusing on the book's message as much as the work you're doing. That's fine when you're only reading for entertainment, but when the book is meant to be teaching something, that can be a problem."

John had never thought about it that way. "Alright, I get it."

"Good." Amy pushed her hair behind her ears. "Since we're on the topic of teaching, have you ever heard of online courses for books?"

John tipped his head in thought. "Like a certification course?"

Amy shook her head. "Let me give you some background. These days many young people are not reading. This is worrisome since these people will soon be in charge of running the world. It was found that many people get information through videos rather than through books. Unfortunately, many of these videos are a mix of bad and good quality. So that's when a publishing company came up with the idea for online courses. This is a short, interesting course where the author teaches you about each of the chapters in their book. They can add extra thoughts, music, and other things to make the video engaging. Each episode is about 20 minutes so as to not lose people's interest."

"I've never heard of anything like this," John said, intrigued.

"We've discovered a lot of benefits. Since the book and course are companions, we've found that 70% of people who buy the book also buy the course. It also works vice versa, sometimes people will discover the course online, and when they finish, they want to buy the book it's based on. This not only brings in more sales and revenue, but it really solidifies the message that the book is aiming to teach.

John liked the sound of that, though a thought occurred to him. "What stops people from listening to the courses while doing other things, the same way they would an audiobook?"

"We also create a study guide to go with the course. This makes people remain present and focus on watching the video."

"I can see how having a visual would also help readers get to know the author better."

"Yes," Amy said, "often when they watch the author speak, it makes them think about how you would be a good speaker in other places. This creates a good opportunity for being invited to speaking engagements or book signings where you can promote your message even further."

"That sounds like an amazing opportunity," John said.

"Would you be interested in doing a course to go a long with your book?"

"Definitely! I'm a bit of a talker anyway."

Amy chuckled. "Well, good. Once you've made your official decision, we'll sort out the details."

As the meeting continued, Amy talked to John about the royalties he could expect. She also let him know that they only retained the rights to his book for five years, after which he could choose to renew or republish elsewhere. This protected his authorial rights in case he didn't like what the company was doing with his book down the line.

"So would you like to accept our offer for publication?" Amy asked as their meeting came to a close.

John hesitated. Despite months of rejections, this all felt like it was happening so fast. Yet the more he heard about this company, the more he felt they were a good fit.

"Yes," he said. "Yes. Let's do this."

"Great! I'll send over a publication agreement for you to look over. If you have any questions or concerns let me know."

The next few months were a blur. The editors were very thorough in their work, and John ended up having to rewrite a few parts, but for the most part it was just a matter of tightening up the word count. The cover was easier since the designer was the one doing all the work; he just had to confirm that he liked it. Some time after that, he got started advertising on his social media. He was sure people were sick of hearing from bhimy the end of it, but he was too excited for the release to care.

The day of the official release he got an email from Amy. *Check your mail,* it said.

John stepped out onto the porch and found a small box on the welcome mat. He immediately brought the box inside.

"Maggie!" he called. "Come look at what just came!"

As his wife entered the room, he was already on the floor using his keys to cut through the tape running down the middle of the box and folded back the cardboard tabs. Amongst the packing paper were 5 new books. A personal copy for himself and three to give away as he pleased. One for Mitch. One for each of his kids. Maybe he should give one to Richard. The thought amused him as he pulled out the first copy and held it gingerly in his hands. He ran his thumb across the pages. He couldn't believe that he'd actually done it. He'd gone from a document on his computer that only a couple other people had read to having his bookstores all across the country.

"Congratulations, honey," Margaret said hugging him around the shoulders.

"Thanks for supporting me through it all," John replied.

For the first time since starting this journey, he let himself think what he hadn't dared put into words.

I'm an author!

～

"Hey, Brian." John leaned back in his office chair, pressing his thumb against the corner of the young man's business card. The card had sat forgotten in his suitcoat pocket for who knew how long, but today, John had happened across it while getting dressed. Brian had said to call if he thought of anymore advice, so he'd decide it could hurt to give the young man a call. "I'm not sure if you remember me, but this is John Larsen."

"Mr. Larsen!" the young man's voice crackled through the speaker in a nervous-excited jitter. "Yes, I remember. I'm still working at your old company. Er…what did you want to talk to me about?"

"Well, a while back, you asked me if I had any business advice for you. I wanted to let you know that I released a book recently on my experiences and methods. I think it could be really helpful for you as you're getting started. It's a lot more detailed than what I was able to share with you back then."

"Yes!" Brian said, "Definitely! I mean, yes, I want to read it. What is it called?"

"The Blueprint to Success. You can buy it on my website or basically any other bookstore."

"Thank you. I'll look it up right away. I've always wanted to start my own business, but I haven't really known how to start."

"I wish you all the luck, Brian. You'll get there. It can just be tough starting out."

"Thanks. Do you have any plans for another project since selling your last business?"

John gazed at the open word document in front of him and smiled. "I think I'll write another book."

Within a few days Brian received John's book. He opened it, and within a few pages, he read the dedication.

Dedicated to Brian, the young man who had so many questions and all who are like him.

"He dedicated his first book to me?" Brian gasped. "No way."

A Note From the Author

This is my 20th published book! For years, I have been encouraging and coaching, inspiring authors to use a storytelling model in their writing. For far too many years, authors have tried to write textbooks for consumers. You know **The 10 things on How to be Successful,** or **The Six Keys to Your Success.** Maybe you've read them. But in the 40 years I have been an entrepreneur, they are often just regurgitated, and honestly boring, ideas celebrating the author.

Fifty-seven percent of the people who purchase a book set it down and never read it again. About a third of the people who watch a webinar or a course turn it off and never return to it.

Why? The author never kept the readers'/viewers' interest. It's boring. It's choppy. It's a talking head.

I hope that if you've made it this far in my little book, you were compelled by the story. What I did here was interweave years of experience in the book publishing world into a fictional story that was entertaining and informative. We followed a story arc, that was developed back in the 16th century. It is the way we in the western world have learned to process story and to expect a journey. That's who John was in this book. He was the author hero. Maybe the things that John experienced you have experienced in your Author journey. If you haven't yet you will. What I've tried to do here is give you a direct path to publishing success.

You can do it.

-Michael

How to Move Forward

After reading this book, you may wonder how you should move forward in your publishing journey. Finding a publisher that fits you, can be difficult, but at Leadership Books we want to help you succeed.

Leadership Books is a traditional publishing company, but unlike most traditional companies, rather than reject books every book that isn't ready, we let authors know when their book has potential. We then give them the option to hire an editor and submit again or to hire one of our in-house editors/coaches to get their book to our publishing standard.

However, there are several other elements that set us apart from other companies.

1. **Unique Coaching.** Leadership Books provides a unique coaching and developmental plan that will help you become not only a published author but a better author. The skill sets that you learn will then help you write your next books. We do offer ghostwriting if needed, however, we believe that your message is told best when it comes from your heart. Take the time to learn, grow, and become better. Just like you need to visit the trainer at the gym to become stronger, as you work with a coach you will

become a better writer. Even though it's hard work, it is worth it.

2. **International Distributors.** We work with a group of international distributors who will make your book available at every level, from retail bookstores to online stores—including Amazon—to our own store. It's important to have a wide, international distribution network for your book because if your book is not widespread, you may struggle. As your popularity grows and your book sells, bookstores will be more likely to carry your book. At Leadership books, we handle all the customer service and distribution. With several warehouses and printing houses around the country, we can ensure that customers will get their books on time.

3. **A Particular Launching Plan.** Over 4 years, we release your books in 4 different publishing types. This is because different groups of people buy different types of books. First, Leadership Books will launch and promote your book as a hardcover. Once your hardcover has sold several hundred copies, we release the paperback book and promote it for about a year. Then we release the ebook and then the audiobook. **We also will create an online course, including a study/discussion guide along with the paperback.**

The life of a book is usually no more than 5 years. Because of this, we only hold copyright for 5 years so that if the booklife runs out, you can take it back, take it out of print, or do whatever you like with it. Though most people decided to keep it in print, we provide that option so that you don't have to buy your own rights back from a publisher. This can be done by sending a simple email when the five years is up.

4. **A Proven Marketing Strategy.** At first, we do what is called intention marketing. This is search engine and google optimization, so when people type in key words looking for a product that your book comes up first. Intention marketing also means doing book signings, getting endorsements, and doing public relations. The intention behind this gets people to click on your landing page. We then retarget all those clicks with a campaign about the course, the book, and the effectiveness of the book. Once they buy book, we continue to retarget that buyer with information about the author as a speaker, business leader, consultant, etc. We do this for 60 days, and in that time, we ask them five times if they would like to meet the author. That can mean taking your mastermind, hiring you as a speaker, hiring you as a consultant, etc.

Basically, what Leadership Books does is take a prospect and turn them into a reader, turn them into a fan, and then turn them into a customer. Our goal is to not only market the book, but to market the author so that your readers have a more permanent relationship with you.

Primarily we use social media, but we also use PR, in person interviews and a lot of other channels, especially in the first 12 weeks of your book, to make your book successful.

5. **We Build Every Part of the Sales Process.** We build every element you need in the sales process you need such as the landing page, automated email campaigns, banner ads, retargeting campaigns, etc. Typically, you would have to hire a complete advertising firm for all that, but we have an internal team to develop everything for you, including developing the online course and implementing the sales process needed to make your book successful.

6. **An Ongoing Coaching Program.** We have an ongoing coaching program and advice program to help you develop your overall business model. For example, if you want to have YouTube channel or a podcast, we can put you in contact with the people who know how to help you. There isn't an area of this business, especially in speaking and consulting, that we don't know somebody who understands how to do it. We are a resource that you can come back to over and over again in our partnership for help. We have a working knowledge in many areas of what works in the field and what doesn't.

7. **Everything Starts With a Book.** Everything we do is to get people to engage with your book. We don't do every part of your marketing, but as your book publisher, we enhance and support your overall marketing process. We want to see how you would like to monetize your book through a podcast, on TV, or public speaking, and help you understand how

to do those things. We have all the proven analytics of what works and doesn't to help. We will be there with you for the entire life cycle of this process, and there's nothing that excites us more than seeing an author succeed.

If you're interested in learning more about publishing a book, developing a course, or Leadership Books in general, set up a Zoom call appointment with our acquisitions team. They will be happy to work with you.

The selection process for taking on books is a simple, two-step process. First, the acquisitions team looks at the book project and idea and determines whether it would be received well in the consumer market. At the same time, they collect a writing sample from you to get a good sense of how you write. If they like it, they'll refer you over to the publishing team and set up a time to talk about the manuscript and what it's going to take to be successful. We love talking to authors, so no agent is required.

Please use this QR code to schedule an appointment. We look forward to meeting you!

Michael's Bio

With over 49 books and training programs to his name, Michael Stickler knows publishing. As an entrepreneur, radio host, and highly sought-after motivational speaker, his expertise and insights have made a strong and transformational impact on the publishing industry. From his best-selling book, A Journey to Generosity (2013), to Cliven Bundy's American Patriot (2017), which is still on the bestseller list, Life Without Reservation (2019), to his latest book Ghost Patriot (2021). Mike continues to drive the publishing market. He has also been the driving factor of Leader Media, Leadership Books' and Leadership Courses success in transforming his corner of the publishing industry.

When Mike isn't shaking up the publishing world, he splits his time between Playa Del Carmen, Mexico, and Lake Tahoe, in the Sierra Nevada foothills, with his wife Faith and their children and grandchildren.